Bolivia

Frontispiece: **Patujú**

Consultant: Miguel Centellas, Department of Sociology and Anthropology, University of Mississippi, Oxford

Please note: All statistics are as up-to-date as possible at the time of publication.

Book production by The Design Lab

Library of Congress Cataloging-in-Publication Data
Names: Yomtov, Nelson, author.
Title: Bolivia / by Nel Yomtov.
Description: New York, NY : Children's Press, an imprint of Scholastic Inc.,
  [2019] | Series: Enchantment of the world | Includes bibliographical
  references and index.
Identifiers: LCCN 2018019516 | ISBN 9780531126943 (library binding)
Subjects: LCSH: Bolivia—Juvenile literature.
Classification: LCC F3308.5 .Y65 2019 | DDC 984—dc23
LC record available at https://lccn.loc.gov/2018019516

Scholastic Inc., 557 Broadway, New York, NY 10012

1 2 3 4 5 6 7 8 9 10 R 28 27 26 25 24 23 22 21 20 19

Bolivia

BY NEL YOMTOV

Enchantment of the World™
Second Series

CHILDREN'S PRESS®

An Imprint of Scholastic Inc.

Contents

Left to right: **Potatoes, Carnival dancer, Sucre, reed boat, Aymara man with wiphala flag**

CHAPTER I

A Land of Contrasts

BOLIVIA IS NICKNAMED THE JEWEL OF THE ANDES. Located in the middle of South America, it is a land of contrasts. The country features snowcapped peaks, arid deserts, fertile plains, and lush rain forests. Looming volcanoes, dried-out prehistoric lakes, and ancient Incan ruins dot the Bolivian landscape.

The country's ethnic and cultural composition is equally striking. Bolivia's population of 11.2 million people is made up of indigenous, or native, people, as well as people of European or African descent. Many Bolivians identify as mestizos, people with a combined European and indigenous heritage. Three main languages are spoken in Bolivia, but the nation officially recognizes more than thirty others. Roman Catholicism is the dominant religion, but many other religions are practiced, including traditional indigenous beliefs.

Opposite: **A young man herds a group of llamas through the mountains of Bolivia. The llama is Bolivia's national animal.**

KEY
- ✪ Capital
- ● Major city
- ○ City
- ■ National park

Cobija
Riberalta○

BRAZIL

PERU

Madidi N.P.

Noel Kempff
Mercado N.P.

San Borja○ ○Trinidad

Lake
Titicaca

○Puerto Acosta

Isiboro Sécure N.P.
and Indigenous Territory

Tiwanaku■ ✪La Paz
Guaqui■ ○El Alto
Achacachi○

BOLIVIA

Coro Coro○

○San Juan de Yapacaní

Cochabamba○ ○Punata
Oruro○

○Aiquile

○Santa Cruz

○Roboré

Isallavi○ ○Llallagua
Chipaya○

○Vallegrande

Kaa-Iya del
Gran Chaco N.P.

Sucre✪ ■Cal Orcko
○Tarabuco

Potosí○

Camiri○

Uyuni○

Aguaragüe
N.P. ○Villamontes

Tupiza○ ○Tarija

PACIFIC
OCEAN

CHILE

Eduardo Avaroa
Andean Fauna Nat'l. Reserve

PARAGUAY

ARGENTINA

NORTH
AMERICA

Area of map

SOUTH
AMERICA

N
W   E
S

0   200 MI
0   200 KM

Historically, Bolivia was home to one of South America's greatest civilizations, the Inca. More than half of Bolivia was part of the immense Incan Empire, which was centered in Peru and stretched from Chile in the south to Colombia in the north along the western edge of the continent.

In the sixteenth century, Spanish conquerors defeated the Incas and seized control of their territories. For more than three centuries, Spanish colonists exploited the land and the native people of Bolivia.

Bolivians finally gained their independence in 1825, after fighting a bloody, fifteen-year war. Political instability frequently marked the years following independence. Short-lived governments and military dictatorships often held power. Over time, Bolivia fought ill-fated wars with neighboring countries and lost more than half of its land.

Bolivia is rich in natural resources, such as crude oil, natural gas, zinc, silver, gold, tin, and lead. Despite its vast economic potential, Bolivia is a poor nation. Many people, especially in rural areas, lack basic sanitation, health care, and education services.

Each year, tens of thousands of people from Bolivia's countryside move to large cities in search of work. Many, however, are unable to find good jobs. They are often forced to live in slums where conditions can be worse than in the rural communities they left.

In recent decades, Bolivia has experienced many positive changes. The nation put valuable social and economic reforms into place in the 1990s. Then, in 2006, Evo Morales became the first indigenous president of Bolivia. Morales introduced reforms that improved the life of the average Bolivian. Progressive programs have improved health care and education. Indigenous groups have been given increased self-rule and equal status to non-indigenous groups. Despite these improvements, Bolivia remains one of the poorest countries in South America. Its greatest challenges are to decrease poverty and achieve long-term economic success.

Bolivia's greatest asset is its people. Diverse, strong, and proud, Bolivians are working to fulfill the promise of creating a brighter future for generations to come.

CHAPTER 2

Peaks, Plains, and Forests

BOLIVIA IS LOCATED IN THE HEART OF THE CONTI-nent of South America. Covering 424,164 square miles (1,098,580 square kilometers), it is about the same size as Texas and California combined.

Bolivia's neighbors are Brazil to the north and east, Paraguay to the southeast, Argentina to the south, and Chile and Peru to the west. Bolivia is landlocked, meaning it has no direct access to the sea. The country can be divided into three geographic regions: the Andes mountain range; the Yungas valleys on the eastern slope of the Andes; and the Oriente, or the tropical lowlands.

Mountains and Altiplano

The Andes mountain range is the world's longest continuous mountain chain. It stretches about 4,500 miles (7,240 km)

Opposite: **Flamingos wade in Laguna Colorada, a lake in southwestern Bolivia famous for its reddish waters.**

along the western length of the South American continent. Studies indicate that the Andes chain was formed twenty-five million years ago. The Andes split into two mountain ranges in western Bolivia. The westernmost range, called the Cordillera Occidental, forms the border with Chile. Peaks in this range have an average elevation of 16,500 feet (5,029 meters) above sea level. At 21,463 feet (6,542 m), Mount Sajama is Bolivia's tallest peak. The Cordillera Occidental receives little precipitation. Most of the region is sparsely populated, and some areas are nearly uninhabited.

A cyclist rides through Sajama National Park. The mountain is an extinct volcano.

Windblown sand has carved a rock into the shape of a tree.

A World of Unearthly Beauty

Bolivia's most visited protected area is the Eduardo Avaroa Andean Fauna National Reserve. Located in the Andes mountains, it covers an area of 2,759 square miles (7,147 sq km). The reserve was created in 1973 to protect the plants, wildlife, and native residents of Bolivia. It was named after Eduardo Abaroa, a Bolivian war hero of the nineteenth century.

The popular reserve is home to an array of colored lakes, bizarre rock formations, snowcapped volcanic peaks, breathtaking deserts, and unforgettable sunsets. Laguna Colorada, the reserve's biggest lake, was once a salt flat. The red algae that live in the shallow water give the lake a bright, otherworldly orange color. Laguna Verde, which lies at the foot of the towering, dormant Licancabur volcano, contains minerals that give the lake greenish hues. Unusual rock formations, some in the shapes of trees, others like the silhouettes of human faces, dot the barren desert

landscapes. The strange formations were carved by windblown sand.

The reserve teems with wildlife. All three South American species of flamingo, as well as eighty other bird species, are found in the reserve. Herds of vicuñas, a relative of the camel, graze on the sparse vegetation. Lucky visitors may catch a glimpse of the rare Andean fox. About two hundred species of plants and trees exist in the reserve. Only hardy vegetation and small shrubs can survive in the harsh terrain and cold temperatures.

Two local communities of indigenous peoples live within the reserve: the Quetena Chico and the Quetena Grande. The communities number roughly seven hundred people in total. Because of the extreme climate of the region, agriculture is impossible. The main economic activities are raising livestock and tourism. Homes are built of adobe with plaster walls inside and mud-covered walls on the outside.

Bolivia's Geographic Features

Highest Elevation: Mount Sajama, 21,463 feet (6,542 m) above sea level

Lowest Elevation: Southeastern border with Paraguay, 295 feet (90 m) above sea level

Longest River: Mamoré, 1,199 miles (1,930 km), forming the border between Bolivia and Brazil

Largest Lake: Lake Titicaca, 3,232 square miles (8,371 sq km)

Longest Border: With Brazil, about 2,000 miles (3,200 km)

Shortest Border: With Paraguay, 468 miles (753 km)

Area: 424,164 square miles (1,098,580 sq km)

Hottest Average Temperature: 86°F (30°C) in the Chaco lowlands

Lowest Average Temperature: 48°F (9°C) in the highlands

Average Annual Precipitation: 39 to 157 inches (100 to 400 cm) in the tropical lowlands; 8 to 31 inches (20 to 79 cm) in the highlands

The eastern range, the Cordillera Oriental, is a series of smaller ranges that run north to south for about 750 miles (1,200 km). The most famous peak is Mount Illimani at 21,122 feet (6,438 m). Towering above the capital city of La Paz, it is a favorite spot for mountain climbers. Large swaths of the Cordillera Oriental are forested and have fertile soil, where fruits and vegetables grow abundantly. Unlike the relatively barren landscape of the Cordillera Occidental, rolling hills and valleys mark the landscape of the Cordillera Oriental.

Alpacas graze the grasslands of the Altiplano. Alpacas are raised for their woolly coats, which can be turned into soft, warm, waterproof yarn.

Between the two ranges lies a vast plateau called the Altiplano. Lying at an average of 12,000 feet (3,700 m) above

sea level, the Altiplano stretches more than 560 miles (900 km) from southern Peru to northern Chile and Argentina. Roughly half of Bolivia's population lives on the Altiplano, the site of the capital city of La Paz.

Because the Andes blocks clouds from reaching the Altiplano, little rain falls in the region. As a result of the dry climate, it has sparse vegetation. Cold nights and biting winds create a harsh environment, especially in the southern part of the plain. The southern Altiplano contains many salt flats, the remains of dried-up lakes. Salar de Uyuni, the largest salt flat in the world, is located in the Altiplano.

The salt crust at Salar de Uyuni ranges in depth from a few inches to 32 feet (10 m).

A person stands in the magical, mirrorlike waters of Salar de Uyuni.

Another World

Salar de Uyuni is the world's largest salt flat. It covers 4,085 square miles (10,580 sq km), making it larger than the states of Delaware and Rhode Island combined. Located on the Altiplano at 11,995 feet (3,656 m) above sea level, it was part of a prehistoric salt lake that once covered much of what is now southwestern Bolivia. When the lake dried up, a vast salt flat was left behind. Salar de Uyuni is estimated to contain more than 10 billion tons of salt, and its top layer is a thick, hard crust that cars can drive on.

An awe-inspiring spectacle, Salar de Uyuni is one of Bolivia's top attractions—and one of the country's most inhospitable landscapes. At night, temperatures there can dip below −13 degrees Fahrenheit (−25 degrees Celsius). During the day, the intense glare from the sun's reflection off the white surface of the salt lake can actually cause snow blindness.

During the rainy season, a thin layer of water covers the salt flats. This forms a highly reflective surface, turning Salar de Uyuni into what is sometimes called "the world's largest mirror." The reflection of the clouds in the vast flatness creates a dreamlike landscape.

The Yungas

To the east of the Cordilleras Oriental are the lush semitropical valleys called the Yungas. The slopes of the Yungas are extremely diverse. Some of the Bolivian Yungas are cloud forests, regions where clouds sit trapped against the Cordilleras Oriental, leaving the forests perpetually damp. Dense forests of hardwood trees thrive here. In the Yungas, fertile soil and abundant rainfall help support the growth of grains, fruits, and coffee. Two of Bolivia's major cities, Cochabamba and Sucre, are located in the Yungas.

The Oriente

The tropical eastern lowlands, the region called the Oriente, cover roughly two-thirds of Bolivia. The northern portion of the Oriente is covered by rain forests, areas with high temperatures and heavy rainfall. Among the many valuable products that come from these humid forests are rubber, Brazil nuts, and cashews.

South of the rain forests, in the central part of the Oriente, lie farmlands and grasslands. Though this part of the lowlands gets less rain than the northern region, its farms produce corn, tobacco, rice, and cotton. Moving eastward, the grasslands stretch to the border of Brazil. Cattle ranching and mining are this area's most important industries. Bolivia's largest city, Santa Cruz, is found in the central portion of the Oriente.

The southernmost region of the Oriente is the Gran Chaco. This area experiences the most dramatic climate shifts in Bolivia. In the early months of the year, the weather is hot with heavy rainfall, which turns the plains into vast swampland. In later months, there is virtually no precipitation at all. The region remains hot, but the grasslands turn dry and dusty.

Lakes and Rivers

Many of Bolivia's major rivers run through the swampy, forested plains of the northeastern Oriente. The northeastward-flowing Beni, Mamoré, Madre de Dios, and Guaporé carry water toward the Amazon River, one of the world's great river systems, which dominates northern South America. In southern and southeastern Bolivia, the Pilcomayo River enters the Gran Chaco, where it forms part of the border with Argentina. Farther south, it joins the Paraguay River and eventually empties into the Atlantic Ocean at the Rio de la Plata. Bolivia's extensive river system provides the major means of transportation throughout the tropical lowlands.

Lake Titicaca, on Bolivia's border with Peru, is one of the world's largest lakes. Lying at an altitude of 12,507 feet (3,812 m) above sea level, Titicaca is the highest navigable body of water on earth. The average depth of the lake ranges between 460 and 600 feet (140 and 180 m), but reaches a depth of 920 feet (280 m) in the lake's northeast corner. Forty-one islands rise from Titicaca's deep, blue waters. The largest, the Island of the Sun, plays an important role in the mythology of the Incas, an indigenous group from western South America.

A man guides a traditional reed boat across Lake Titicaca.

The Legend of Manco Cápac

The Manco Kapac Province is located in western Bolivia, on the border of Lake Titicaca. The province was named for Manco Cápac, the founder of the Inca dynasty. According to legend, Manco Cápac was the child of the sun god, Inti, who sent him to earth at the Island of the Sun. Manco Cápac led his people into Peru. There he founded Cuzco, the Incan capital.

Manco Cápac is considered the founder of the Inca civilization.

Climate

Bolivia is located in the tropics—the region of earth that lies near the equator, around the middle of the globe. Situated in the Southern Hemisphere, Bolivia's seasons are the opposite of those in the Northern Hemisphere. In Bolivia, summer runs from December to May and winter from June to November.

The weather in the highlands is normally dry and cold. In the higher reaches of the Andes, temperatures range from 41°F to 59°F (5°C to 15°C) during the day and from 23°F to 14°F (–5°C to –10°C) at night. There is snow in the Andes year-round at elevations above about 15,000 feet (4,600 m). Peaks at more than 18,000 feet (5,500 m) have glaciers on them.

Mount Illimani looms over Bolivia's capital city of La Paz. The glaciers on the mountain are a vital source of water for the city.

An Alarming Shortage

In late 2016, the government of Bolivia declared a state of emergency after the worst drought in twenty-five years affected several of the country's major cities, including the capital, La Paz. The water shortage forced officials to institute a widespread program of water rationing that continues today. Experts claim the drought is largely due to climate change and disappearing glaciers. More than two million Bolivians rely on glacial meltwater for drinking and cooking purposes. Meltwater is also needed for irrigation and hydropower.

As the world warms because human activity is sending more greenhouse gases into the atmosphere, trapping heat near the earth, Bolivia's mountain glaciers are disappearing at an alarming rate. According to one study, between 1986 and 2014, the glaciers of Bolivia shrank by 43 percent. Worldwide changing weather patterns and poor water management by the government have also contributed to Bolivia's water woes.

In the Altiplano, average high temperatures range from 60°F to 70°F (16°C to 21°C) during the day. At nighttime, temperatures can drop as low as 6°F (–14°C). Farther south, in regions such as the Uyuni salt flats, temperatures vary widely. Most of the Altiplano receives 20 to 25 inches (51 to 64 centimeters) of rain annually. The southern region, however, has extremely arid conditions. Annual rainfall there is frequently less than 5 inches (13 cm) per year.

Bolivia's tropical lowlands have daytime high temperatures of around 86°F (30°C) year-round. High humidity and heavy

Clouds hang among the mountains of the Yungas.

In 2011, a landslide caused by heavy rain buckled roads and destroyed houses in La Paz. Twenty-five thousand people were left homeless.

rainfall are typical with most areas receiving at least 60 inches (152 cm) of rain each year. In some years, the rainy season of late September to May brings as much as 150 inches (380 cm) of rain. Destructive mudslides sometimes kill people and destroy houses. The heavy rainfall occurs when winds carry humid air in from the Amazon rain forest.

Farther south, in the Chaco region, the climate is more arid. Annual rainfall averages 20 to 40 inches (50 to 100 cm) annually. From September to November, temperatures can often reach 104°F (40°C), while between May and August temperatures can drop to freezing.

Urban Landscapes

With an estimated population of about 1.5 million people, Santa Cruz is the largest city in Bolivia. Located in the tropical lowlands, it is the hub of Bolivia's economy, with thriving oil, gas, timber, food processing, and cattle industries. Santa Cruz was founded in 1561. Visitors enjoy sites such as San Lorenzo Cathedral, which was built in the 1800s and features exquisite silverwork and a bell tower people are permitted to climb.

El Alto is the nation's second-largest city, home to roughly 850,000. El Alto is located right next to Bolivia's capital and third-largest city, La Paz, which has a population approaching 800,000. Together they are the nation's largest metropolitan area. Throughout much of its history, El Alto was a small suburb of La Paz, and it was not incorporated as a city until 1987. Today, it is the nation's fastest-growing city, known for its clogged streets.

Cochabamba, Bolivia's fourth-largest city, has a population of about 630,000. Lying in

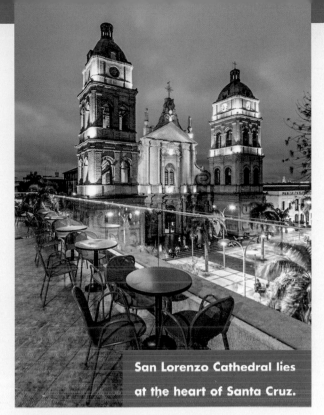

San Lorenzo Cathedral lies at the heart of Santa Cruz.

a fertile valley in the center of the country, Cochabamba is the economic heart of Bolivia's main agricultural region. The city is renowned for its sprawling marketplace known as La Cancha. It is also home to the Archaeological Museum, which boasts an extensive collection of items representing pre-Spanish culture.

About 265,000 people live in Oruro, Bolivia's fifth-largest city. Founded by the Spaniards in 1606, Oruro is located on the Altiplano south of La Paz. Oruro was long the center of Bolivia's richest tin-mining region. When world tin prices plummeted in the 1980s, the city slipped into economic decline. Since then, Oruro has developed a strong tourist industry. It now serves as a stopover for visitors who want to take in nearby natural and archaeological wonders. The city is famed for its spectacular Carnival.

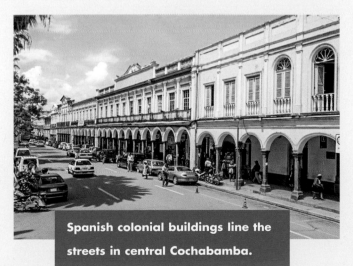

Spanish colonial buildings line the streets in central Cochabamba.

CHAPTER 3

Nature's Bounty

BOLIVIA'S VARIED GEOGRAPHY AND RANGE OF CLI-
mates make it one of the most biologically diverse
countries on earth. Bolivia contains about 2,900
animal species, including 1,350 species of birds, nearly 500
species of amphibians and reptiles, and more than 600 species
of fish. Amazingly, new species of wildlife are discovered each
year. In 2015, seven new animal species and ten new plant
species were found in Madidi National Park, one of the largest
preserved areas in the country.

In the Highlands

The cold, dry, and windy conditions of the highlands limit the
number of animal and plant species that can survive there.
Cacti, scrub grasses, brush, and scanty trees are the most common plants found in the highlands. Andean bunch grass, or

Opposite: **The brown-
throated sloth is one of
more than three hundred
species of mammals that
live in Bolivia. The sloth's
long claws help it hang
from branches, even
while asleep.**

Red-and-green macaws fly above the trees in Madidi National Park. It is estimated that 11 percent of the world's bird species can be found in the park.

Spectacular Diversity

Madidi National Park in western Bolivia is believed to be the most diverse national park on earth. Covering an area nearly the size of the U.S. state of New Jersey, Madidi rises from an elevation of 600 feet (200 m) to 20,000 feet (6,000 m). It features cloud forests, wetlands, and Andean peaks. These diverse habitats contain an incredible array of life.

More than a thousand bird species live in the park, a larger number than is found in all of the United States. The park is home to more than 250 species of mammals, including jaguars, sloths, and dolphins. In addition, roughly a thousand species of butterfly have been identified in Madidi, with more still being discovered.

ichu, grows in the mountains and highland meadows. This tough grass has traditionally been used to make adobe, which is dried mud brick that contains straw. Ichu is also used as thatch on the roofs of traditional homes.

Drought-adapted queñua trees and eucalyptus trees can survive the harsh conditions of the highlands. One of Bolivia's national flowers, the kantuta, grows abundantly in the rocky Andes. Among other species that grow in the high Andes are the totora, a type of bulrush used to make reed mats and boats, and the yareta, a plant harvested for fuel.

Climate conditions in these higher elevations also limit the kinds of crops that can be grown. Potatoes and oca, another root vegetable, have been the major source of food for dwellers on the Altiplano for hundreds of years. The potato originated in the Andes. More than four thousand varieties of potato are grown in the Andean highlands of Bolivia, Peru,

Cacti grow in the arid landscape of southern Bolivia.

and Ecuador. The oca root is eaten like the potato—boiled, baked, or fried.

The highlands are home to a limited number of animals. These include llamas, alpacas, guanacos, and vicuñas. These are all camelids, animals related to camels. Llamas are used as beasts of burden and their meat can be eaten fresh or dried to make jerky. The wool of all four animals is used to make clothing. Other animals that live in the highlands include Andean foxes,

Cougars are one of the largest predators in Bolivia. They hunt by ambush, lying quietly until their prey comes near, before they pounce.

The kantuta grows on a thick evergreen shrub.

The nectar of the patujú attracts many birds, especially hummingbirds.

Bolivia's National Flowers

Bolivia has two national flowers, the kantuta and the patujú. Each represents a different region of the country. The kantuta is native to the western highlands. Often called the Sacred Flower of the Incas, it is tiny and fragile. It is red, yellow, and green. The patuju hails from the eastern tropics. It is very large with red, yellow, and green flowers facing downward. Because of the patujú's shape and dominant red color, it is sometimes known as hanging lobster claw.

pumas, and large, ostrich-like birds called rheas. The Andean condor soars in the skies above the highlands. Pink flamingos and other waterbirds make their home at Laguna Colorada in the Eduardo Avaroa Andean Fauna National Reserve.

Andean condors are scavengers, feeding on the meat of dead animals. They have excellent eyesight, which allows them to spy food while gliding high above the land.

The National Bird

The Andean condor is Bolivia's national bird. Among the world's largest flying birds, the majestic Andean condor stands more than 4 feet (1.2 m) tall and has a wingspan of 10 feet (3 m). Weighing as much as 33 pounds (15 kilograms), it is the world's heaviest bird of prey. Most condors are black, with males having a white band around their necks and white markings on their wings. Condors belong to the vulture family and feed on the bodies of large dead animals. Among the longest-living birds, Andean condors have been known to live more than seventy years.

In the Yungas

Wildlife in the semitropical foothills of the Yungas includes jaguars, ocelots, spectacled bears, tapirs, and different types of monkey. Deer, caimans, and capybaras, the largest living rodent in the world, also live here. In the skies soar giant hummingbirds, macaws, ospreys, toucans, and whistling herons. Roughly 90 percent of the animals that are found only in Bolivia make their home in the Yungas.

Plant life in the Yungas ranges from tall grasses and low shrubs to forests of ferns and bamboo. Other plant life includes cedar trees and the cinchona plant. Cedar wood is used in outdoor construction, fences, and furniture. The bark of the cinchona plant is used to make quinine, a medicine used to treat diseases, such as malaria.

The coca plant thrives in the Yungas. The plant grows on slopes between roughly 1,600 and 4,200 feet (500 and 1,300 m)

Capybaras are related to guinea pigs but are the size of a large dog. They are highly social animals, often living in large groups.

Thousands of different plant species live in the rain forest of Bolivia.

high. For centuries, Bolivians have used the plant to brew tea and have chewed the coca leaf. Coca helps relieve the symptoms of living in the thin air of the highlands, such as dizziness and headaches. Incan healers used the coca plant to make medicine to treat a variety of ailments. The coca plant, however, is also used to produce cocaine, a harmful, addictive drug.

In the Lowlands

The rain forests in Bolivia's northern lowlands stretch into the Amazon River basin of Brazil. The major rivers that feed the mighty Amazon—the Madeira, Mamoré, Madre de Dios, Manuripi, and Beni— cross the region. One can best observe the rich diversity of plant and animal life in the lowlands along the rivers.

Roughly six hundred kinds of trees grow in this region. Among the giant trees are the kapok and the Brazil nut. Kapoks can grow up to 13 feet (4 m) a year, and reach a height of 165 feet (50 m). The Brazil nut tree grows as tall as the kapok and may live for five hundred years or more. The seed of the tree, commonly called the Brazil nut, is an excellent source of nutrition. Bolivia produces approximately 45 percent of the world's supply of Brazil nuts.

In the rain forest, the thick, tall growth of trees prevents sunlight from reaching the forest floor. Woody vines, called lianas, grow up tree trunks to reach light. Mosses, orchids, ferns, and bromeliads grow on many of the lowland trees.

Rain forest animal life is equally abundant. Sloths, armadillos, capybaras, pumas, and jaguars roam the forest floor. A variety of monkeys also live in the rain forest. These include squirrel monkeys, red howlers, and spider monkeys. Many colorful birds live in the region, including roseate spoonbills, macaws, storks, parrots, and parakeets.

Anacondas and caimans are found along the water's edge. More than two thousand species of fish live in the waters of the Amazon basin. Kinds of fish living in the Amazon include catfish, electric eel, stingray, and piranha. The Bolivian river dolphin, called *bufeos*, is rare and found only in the upper Madeira River basin.

Moving south, tall grasses and low shrubs dominate the landscape. Corn, soybeans, and sorghum are grown on the plowed fields. Wildlife is limited, but includes species found in the tropics, such as caimans and capybaras.

Animal and plant life in the Gran Chaco have adapted to the harsh environment. Despite its arid conditions, the Chaco is home to more than three thousand plant species,

Some species of pencil catfish feed by swimming into the gills of larger fish. They chew on the fish gills, eating the blood.

Pencil Catfishes

Seven species of catfish are found only in Bolivia. Some are long and thin and are commonly known as pencil catfishes. One species of Bolivian catfish is found in the Apere River, a tributary of the Mamoré River. This species grows to a maximum length of nearly 12 inches (30 cm).

A smaller species, which grows less than 2 inches (5 cm) long, inhabits the Paraná River system in the Aguaragüe National Park. Young catfish feed on insects such as water beetles and fly larvae. As they become adults, their diet includes plants, algae, and snails.

five hundred species of birds, and 150 species of mammals. Animals include pumas, giant anteaters, armadillos, and peccaries, or wild pigs. Only plants and trees that can survive with little water grow in the Chaco. A dry forest of thorny shrubs and low trees grows in the west.

The Gran Chaco stretches from Bolivia into Paraguay. It is South America's second-largest wilderness, trailing only the Amazon rain forest. In recent years, the natural habitats of the Bolivian Chaco have been disrupted. A gas pipeline and military operations have destroyed part of the environment. Erika Cuéllar, a Bolivian biologist, is teaching indigenous people to collect data on the wildlife living in the Gran Chaco and to present it to conservationists. "These people are a part of the natural environment; they belong to this land," she said. "If they are not involved, I don't see how we can achieve the long-term conservation of the biodiversity of this area."

The main foods of the southern anteater are ants, termites, and honey. It uses its long snout and tongue to reach into insect nests.

CHAPTER 4

Conquest and Independence

Historians believe that the earliest human settlements in the region that is now Bolivia date back to before 10,000 BCE. These early peoples settled in the Andes.

At first, the people moved about, hunting game and gathering wild plants to eat. Over the centuries, they gradually settled into farming communities, where they grew cotton, corn, and potatoes. These early people also domesticated animals and herded llamas for meat and wool.

By 1500 BCE, permanent settlements were well established on the eastern slopes of the Andes and in the Altiplano. Around this time, people also began to reside on the southern shores of Lake Titicaca, especially around what became the city of Tiwanaku. It was there that Bolivia's first great civilization was born.

Opposite: **The Tiwanaku people carved monumental figures from stone. Some of these figures were more than 20 feet (6 m) tall.**

The Tiwanaku

Between 100 BCE and 600 CE, the Tiwanaku culture dominated the region around Lake Titicaca. The powerful empire stretched from Bolivia into Peru and Chile. At its height, the capital city of Tiwanaku had a population of fifty thousand people.

The Tiwanaku people were master builders and engineers. They constructed extensive networks of paved roads that connected their colonies on the western coast of South America to the highlands and tropical valleys farther east. They erected huge structures—temples, gateways, and walls—with enormous stone slabs, skillfully decorated with carved figures and animals. Canals that carried water for irrigation were erected across the fields on which farmers grew corn and other crops.

The Tiwanaku people were also skilled metalworkers and astronomers. They learned how to smelt tin and copper to make bronze. They also studied the skies and the movement of the sun to create an accurate calendar.

By 1200 CE, the Tiwanaku civilization disappeared. The reason for its collapse is uncertain. Recent evidence indicates a long drought may have caused crops to fail, causing starvation. If this was the case, the Tiwanaku would have been forced to leave their city.

The Tiwanaku culture was succeeded by the Aymara people. The Aymara were divided into several groups that lived in Bolivia and Peru. Modern Bolivian Aymara are the descendants of these ancient peoples. The most dominant Aymara kingdoms were based around Lake Titicaca. The lack of unity among the different Aymara communities, however,

Tourists look at some of the thousands of giant dinosaur footprints at Cal Orcko.

Wall of the Giants

Cal Orcko, located near Sucre in the southern highlands, is home to the world's largest and most diverse collection of dinosaur footprints. The tracks date to sixty-eight million years ago. In 1985, workers for a cement company unearthed the first footprints while mining limestone. In 1994, scientific excavations revealed a giant limestone wall covered in dinosaur tracks. The wall contains more than five thousand footprints made by fifteen different types of dinosaurs. One of the most interesting tracks is the one left by a baby *Tyrannosaurus rex* that extends more than 1,100 feet (335 m). The 260-foot-tall (79 m) wall rises at a steep incline from the ground. Due to movements below the ground, the once-horizontal limestone surface has been pushed up into a vertical position. Visitors can take a tour to the edge of the wall for a close look at the amazing prehistoric impressions.

left them unable to defend themselves when the Inca people from the north invaded.

The Incan Empire

In the 1430s, Incan armies swept into western Bolivia. By the 1460s, they had conquered all of the Aymara kingdoms. Originally from the Cuzco Valley in Peru, the Incas seized region after region. Like the Tiwanaku, the Incas were extraordinary engineers. They built magnificent cities, bridges, irrigation canals, terraced farms, and vast networks of roadways. Artisans produced colorful textiles and made stunning objects in ceramic, gold, and

The Incas built large cities in their empire, including Machu Picchu, which was located high in the mountains of Peru.

silver. The Inca spoke a language called Quechua, which they taught to their conquered subjects. In Bolivia, however, the Inca allowed their subjects to continue speaking Aymara. This language continues to be spoken in parts of Bolivia and elsewhere in South America.

By 1500, the Incan Empire stretched more than 4,000 miles (6,400 km) north to south, from what is now northern Ecuador to southern Chile. At its height, the empire was home to more than ten million people.

AYMARA KINGDOMS, 14th CENTURY

CANCHIS
CANAS
COLLAS
SORAS
LUPACAS
PACAJES
CHARCAS
CHUIS
CARACARAS
CARANGAS
QUILLACAS
CHICHAS
PACIFIC OCEAN

KEY
— Present-day Bolivia

The Spanish Invasion

In 1532, Spanish adventurers Francisco Pizarro and Diego de Almagro arrived in Peru with 180 soldiers called conquistadores. The Spaniards had come in search of gold and silver, which they were determined to obtain by any means. Pizarro soon encountered the Incan leader, Atahualpa. Pizarro hatched a plan to ambush Atahualpa and capture him. On November 16, 1532, Pizarro's conquistadores attacked Incan warriors with cannons, crossbows, swords, and lances. The Spaniards killed more than a thousand Incas and took Atahualpa captive. The Incas paid the Spaniards a ransom of 13,420 pounds of gold and 26,000 pounds of silver. Nevertheless, Pizarro had Atahualpa executed. Spanish control of the Andes had begun.

Establishing a Colonial Empire

In the years following the execution of Atahualpa, Pizarro and his armies continued to conquer Incan territories. Indigenous people were forced from their ancestral homes and relocated to towns near agricultural centers. There the Spaniards used the native people as laborers on farms. To convert the people to Christianity, the Spaniards built churches in many regions.

Francisco Pizarro led the conquest of Peru in 1532. He spent the rest of his life trying to maintain his family's power there.

The Jesuit Missions of Chiquitos mixed architectural styles from Europe with indigenous designs.

Jesuit Missions of Chiquitos

The Jesuit Missions of Chiquitos in eastern Bolivia were created in the seventeenth and eighteenth centuries. They served as *reducciones de indios*—settlements where Jesuit priests converted indigenous people to Christianity. Eleven missions were built between 1691 and 1760. The missions housed thousands of people. Each mission featured a large plaza used for religious and civil purposes, and a complex that included a church, workshops, living quarters, schools, and a vegetable garden. The buildings were constructed in a unique blend of European and local architecture.

Over time, the Jesuits became wealthy and powerful. Spanish kings resented their influence in the colony. In 1767, the Spanish monarchy expelled the Jesuits from all Spanish territories. The six settlements in Chiquitos are the only Jesuit missions in South America that were not destroyed after the Jesuits were expelled. The Chiquitos missions are one of Bolivia's most popular tourist attractions.

Veins of silver ran through Cerro Rico ("rich mountain"), which looms over the city of Potosí. The city was Spain's largest silver supplier during the colonial era.

In 1543, the Spaniards established the Viceroyalty of Peru, the official name of their new colonial empire. The center of government was set up in Lima, Peru. The territory that included Bolivia was called Upper Peru. In the following decades, the Spaniards founded colonial Bolivia's most important cities, including La Paz, Santa Cruz, and Chuquisaca, which was later named Sucre.

Vast Riches

In 1544, a rich silver deposit was discovered at the Cerro Rico mountain in the Andes. The following year, the city of Potosí was founded at the foot of the mountain. To extract the valuable metal, the Spaniards enslaved indigenous people and forced them to work in the underground mines. Thousands died each year from starvation, accidents, disease, and strenuous work. The output of the Potosí mines was staggering. More than $1.5 billion worth of silver was sent to Spain in the first three decades of mining. The population of Potosí swelled to nearly two hundred thousand people, more than London or Paris at the time.

Meanwhile, the Spaniards established large plantations on which the native people were put to work. Much of the land was illegally taken from the indigenous people. The cost to them was terrible, and many were furious at their European overlords.

The Spanish packed silver into trunks such as this to be shipped back to Europe. Over the course of two hundred years, more than 40,000 tons of silver were shipped out of Potosí.

Pedro Domingo Murillo was a leader in the movement for independence from Spain in 1809. He was executed in La Paz the following year.

Independence!

Far from what is now Bolivia, political and social conditions were changing rapidly. The American and French revolutions of the 1700s inspired notions of independence among the people of Upper Peru. When the French invaded Spain and overthrew the Spanish monarchy in 1808, colonists took action. The following year, people in Chuquisaca and La Paz proclaimed independence from Spain.

But independence was not yet won. For fifteen years, people in Upper Peru battled each other and royalist forces in the War of Independence. Guerrilla groups supporting independence from Spain gained control of six different areas of the countryside, which became known as *republiquetas*, or little republics.

Meanwhile, other parts of South America were also fighting for independence. Venezuelan-born Simón Bolívar was one of the leaders of this independence movement. He sought independence not only for Bolivia, but for Colombia, Ecuador, Peru, and Venezuela as well. In December 1824, Bolívar's lieutenant, General Antonio José de Sucre, defeated the Spaniards at the Battle of Ayacucho in Peru. On August 6, 1825, Bolivia was declared a republic.

The New Nation

The new republic named itself Bolivia in honor of Simón Bolívar, the "Great Liberator." Bolívar served as the nation's first president, but only for a few months. In January 1826, General Sucre was elected as the first constitutional president of Bolivia. Sucre introduced a series of programs aimed at achieving greater equality for all Bolivians. He began

INDEPENDENCE FROM SPAIN

PERU
1821

BRAZIL
(Independent from
Portugal 1822)

BOLIVIA
1825

PARAGUAY
1811

UNITED
PROVINCES
OF THE RÍO
DE LA PLATA
1816

URUGUAY
1828

CHILE
1818

KEY
■ Spanish territory in 1810
1825 Date of independence
— Present-day Bolivia

Túpac Katari

Túpac Katari of the Aymara led a major revolt to drive the Spanish out of Bolivia and establish self-rule by the indigenous population. Born Julián Apaza Nina around 1750, he took the name Túpac Katari ("resplendent serpent" in the Aymara language). In 1781, Katari, his wife, his sister, and an army of about forty thousand other Aymaras laid siege to La Paz for six months. The rebels destroyed churches and government property, but the Spaniards eventually crushed the uprising. Katari was captured and executed. Today, Katari is considered a cultural hero, an Aymara martyr who gave his life for the cause of indigenous independence. Moments before his death, he is believed to have said, "I alone shall die, but I will return in millions and millions."

Túpac Katari took his name to honor earlier Aymara leaders.

taxing wealthy plantation owners and seizing their estates. Sucre reduced the power of the Roman Catholic Church and tried to reform the tax system. After a failed coup—one of nearly two hundred in Bolivia between 1825 and 1981—Sucre resigned.

Bolivia's second president, Andrés de Santa Cruz, was the nation's first Bolivian-born leader. He established universities at La Paz and Cochabamba and balanced the state budget to make Bolivia debt-free. When civil war erupted in Peru, Santa Cruz ordered Bolivian armies to invade. The following year, he forced a union of the two nations. Argentina and Chile opposed the move. Together with Peru they eventually defeated Bolivian forces at the Battle of Yungay in 1839. Santa Cruz was exiled to France.

Internal Strife and Costly Wars

Decades of regional feuds and rivalries between military officers and landowners followed in the wake of the humiliating defeat at Yungay. The internal strife crippled the Bolivian economy and destroyed any sense of national unity.

From 1879 to 1883, Bolivia fought Chile in the War of the Pacific over Bolivian lands along the coast. Bolivia lost the war and was forced to give Chile these mineral-rich lands. Losing these lands also meant that Bolivia lost access to the Pacific Ocean. Bolivia was now a landlocked nation, forcing it to become dependent on the ports of neighboring Chile and Peru.

WAR OF THE PACIFIC

PERU

BOLIVIA

PACIFIC OCEAN

CHILE

ARGENTINA

KEY
— Boundaries, 1874
■ Territory lost to Chile, 1874
■ Territory lost to Chile, 1884
— Present-day boundaries

Between 1932 and 1935, Bolivia was at war again, this time with Paraguay. When rumors of oil in the Gran Chaco surfaced in the late 1920s, the two nations began to dispute the position of the border. Known as the Chaco War, it cost the lives of eighty thousand Bolivians and hundreds of millions of dollars. Bolivia lost territory in the Chaco, and in the end, no oil was discovered there.

A Turning Point

The Chaco War signaled the need for social and economic change in Bolivia. Stirred by feelings of nationalism, indigenous peoples and the descendants of Spaniards joined together to bring about major reforms.

The Nationalist Revolutionary Movement (MNR) sprang up as a major political party in the 1940s. In 1952, with the support of mine workers and peasants, Víctor Paz Estenssoro, the MNR candidate, won the presidency. A military coup, however, blocked Paz Estenssoro from taking office. His supporters were outraged, and an MNR-sponsored armed revolt erupted in April 1952. The military was defeated, and Paz Estenssoro became president.

The new leader launched a program of land reform that broke up large estates and returned them to their original owners, the indigenous people. Also, all Bolivian adults were given the right to vote, and education and social welfare programs were promoted.

From 1952 to 1964, Bolivia made enormous progress as a developing democratic nation. The economy, however, was

weak, and the MNR began to splinter into different groups with competing interests.

Bolivian troops march through La Paz during the Chaco War.

Political Turmoil

In 1964, a military coup ousted Paz Estenssoro as he began his third presidential term. In 1966, one of the military officers who participated in the coup, General René Barrientos Ortuño, was elected president. Barrientos ruled as a dictator,

Fighting for Rights

Luis Espinal was a Spanish-born Jesuit priest who fought for democracy and human rights. Born in 1932 in Catalonia, Spain, Espinal came to Bolivia in 1968 to head the journalism department at the Catholic University in La Paz. He became a filmmaker, producing documentaries on social themes and political conditions in Bolivia. Espinal helped organize hunger strikes to protest human rights violations being committed by the regime of President Hugo Bánzer Suárez.

In 1979, Espinal founded the newpaper *Aquí* (Here), which published information about government corruption and the military's involvement in drug trafficking. On March 21, 1980, Father Espinal was kidnapped by a government death squad. He was tortured and killed, and his body was thrown into a landfill. Bolivians were outraged. More than seventy thousand Bolivians attended his burial. In death, Father Espinal became a national hero and a Bolivian martyr in the fight for freedom.

and his administration was plagued by labor unrest. That same year, left-wing revolutionary Ernesto "Che" Guevara tried to organize an uprising to overthrow Barrientos. Guevara's attempt failed when he was captured and killed by the Bolivian army in October 1967.

After Barrientos's death in 1969, the government was unstable. One leader after another was forced from office. Among them was a series of military leaders who imprisoned and tortured their opponents to maintain power. In 1979, the Bolivian legislature appointed Lidia Gueiler Tejada interim president until elections could be held, making her the nation's first female president. Within months, however, General Luis García Meza seized power in a bloody coup. The dictator outlawed all political parties, censored the media, and exiled opposition leaders. After Meza was linked to the illegal drug trade, his oppressive administration was overthrown.

Democracy Again

Since 1982, Bolivia has experienced the longest period of democratically elected government in its history. In 1985, Víctor Paz Estenssoro assumed the presidency once again. He launched a program called the New Economic Policy, or NPE. Under the program, Paz Estenssoro helped bring the nation's soaring inflation under control. Working with U.S. troops, he slashed Bolivia's trade in illegal drugs. Political and economic stability had returned to Bolivia.

Víctor Paz Estenssoro (front center, in hat) dominated Bolivian politics in the mid-twentieth century.

General Hugo Bánzer Suárez, leader of the Nationalist Democratic Action (ADN) party was elected president in 1997. Bánzer, a former dictator who held the presidency from 1971 to 1978, had come to embrace democratic politics. He negotiated new trade agreements and encouraged foreign investment in Bolivia, which further helped improve Bolivia's economy.

Recent Times

In 2000, a protest in the city of Cochabamba erupted into a deadly conflict known as the Water War. President Bánzer had agreed to sell Bolivia's water company to a group of international investors. The major investor was the U.S.-based Bechtel Corporation. When the new owners raised water delivery rates, residents of Cochabamba became outraged. Violent protests broke out, resulting in the deaths of seven citizens. Eventually, the company gave up its water interests, and Cochabamba took control of its own water system.

Riots erupted again in 2003, this time over the country's vast natural gas reserves. Bolivian reserves are the second largest in South America, after Venezuela. The state-owned national oil company could not afford to tap into the reserves. The Bolivian government granted a license to British and Spanish companies to exploit the resource. Many groups in Bolivia opposed foreign involvement in the country's natural resources. Protests escalated into bloody confrontations with Bolivian armed forces. Dozens of people were killed or wounded. Both President Gonzalo Sánchez de Lozada and his successor, Carlos Mesa Gisbert, were forced to resign because of the ongoing violent protests.

In the 2005 elections, Evo Morales won 54 percent of the vote and became the first indigenous president of Bolivia. In one of his first official declarations, Morales decreed that most natural gas reserves would become owned by the state. Morales also launched a movement to improve education among indigenous groups and encouraged schools to teach native languages such as Aymara and Quechua. Morales's programs have helped reduce poverty and increase literacy in Bolivia, and he won reelection in 2009 and again in 2014.

In 2003, protests broke out as Bolivians demanded that the government take control of the nation's natural gas reserves.

CHAPTER 5

Democracy at Work

SINCE BOLIVIA DECLARED ITS INDEPENDENCE IN 1825, the nation has had seventeen constitutions. The latest constitution, adopted in 2009, officially changed the name of the Republic of Bolivia to the Plurinational State of Bolivia. *Plurinational* means that multiple ethnic groups and cultures exist in the country and that all groups participate in the government. The new constitution defines Bolivia as a "social Unitarian state." According to Article 4, Bolivia is a secular nation, rather than a Catholic one, as it had been previously.

Similar to the United States, Bolivia's federal government has three branches: executive, legislative, and judicial.

Executive Branch

The executive branch of government consists of the president, the vice president, and the ministers of state. The president

Opposite. **An Aymara man holds a wiphala flag, which represents the indigenous people of the Andes. It is officially the dual flag of Bolivia.**

The National Flag

The flag of Bolivia was officially adopted in 1851.

The Bolivian flag consists of three horizontal stripes of red, yellow, and green. Red symbolizes the blood of Bolivia's brave soldiers, yellow is for Bolivia's wealth and resources, and green stands for fertility and the nation's natural beauty. When flown by the government of Bolivia, the flag includes the national coat of arms in the center. The coat of arms includes symbols of Bolivia, including a condor, Mount Potosí, and an alpaca.

and vice president must belong to the same political party. If the president resigns or dies in office, he or she is replaced by the vice president.

The president and vice president are elected by popular vote to five-year terms. Under the 2009 constitution, they were limited to two terms. In 2016, Bolivians voted on a constitutional amendment that would have ended presidential term limits. Voters rejected the amendment, keeping the two-term limit in place. The following year, however, the nation's Constitutional Court ended term limits, ruling that they violated the candidates' human rights.

The president is both the head of state and the head of government. The president conducts foreign affairs; oversees security and defense; and appoints the ministers of state, the attorney general, and high-ranking military officials. He or she also works with the legislature to make laws and proposes the budget.

The president of Bolivia directs more than twenty ministries, or departments, which supervise the day-to-day functioning of the nation. The executive cabinet is made up of the heads of each of the ministries, called ministers. The ministries include the Ministry of Defense, Education, Health, Economy and Finance, Energies, Mining, and Sports.

Legislative Branch

Bolivia's legislative branch is made up of two houses that create the nation's laws: the Chamber of Deputies and the Chamber of Senators. The Chamber of Deputies has 130 members. Seventy deputies are elected by popular vote. Fifty-

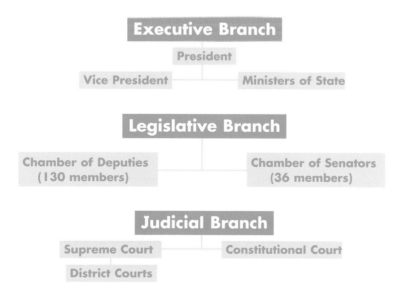

National Government of Bolivia

The National Anthem

"Bolivianos, el Hado Propicio" ("Bolivians, a Most Favorable Destiny") is the national anthem of Bolivia. It was written by José Ignacio de Sanjinés and composed by an Italian, Leopoldo Benedetto Vincenti. The anthem was adopted in 1851.

Spanish lyrics

Bolivianos: el hado propicio
coronó nuestros votos y anhelos.
Es ya libre, ya libre este suelo,
ya cesó su servil condición.
Al estruendo marcial que ayer fuera
y al clamor de la guerra horroroso,
siguen hoy, en contraste armonioso,
dulces himnos de paz y de unión.
Siguen hoy, en contraste armonioso,
dulces himnos de paz y de unión.

De la Patria, el alto nombre,
en glorioso esplendor conservemos.
Y en sus aras de nuevo juremos:
¡Morir antes que esclavos vivir!
¡Morir antes que esclavos vivir!
¡Morir antes que esclavos vivir!

English translation

Bolivians, a favorable fate
As at long last crowned our vows and longings;
This land is free, free at last.
Its servile state has now finally ceased.
The martial turmoil of yesterday,
And the horrible clamor of war,
Are followed today, in harmonious contrast,
By sweet hymns of peace and unity.

Let us keep the lofty name of our Fatherland
In glorious splendor.
And, on its altars, once more we must swear:
To die before we would live as slaves!
To die before we would live as slaves!
To die before we would live as slaves!

three deputies are elected by proportional representation. In this form of electoral system, people vote for a particular party. That party is then given the same percentage of seats as it won in the election. Seven seats in the Chamber of Deputies are reserved for indigenous representatives.

The Chamber of Senators has thirty-six members. Each of Bolivia's nine departments, regional divisions similar to states, selects four senators. Deputies and senators are elected to five-year terms.

The Chamber of Senators and Chamber of Deputies meet in a historic building on Plaza Murillo, in the center of La Paz.

A Pair of Capitals

Bolivia is one of fifteen countries in the world with two capitals. Located on the eastern edge of the Altiplano, Sucre is the constitutional and legal capital. La Paz is the seat of government, where the executive and legislative branches of government are located. After Bolivia achieved independence in 1825, Sucre was made the capital, with all three branches of government residing there. In 1898, the presidency and the legislature were moved to La Paz. Sucre remained the seat of the Supreme Court and the judicial branch.

Sucre is home to about 250,000 people. The city center contains many historic buildings, such as the House of Freedom, where the Bolivian Act of Independence was signed on August 6, 1825. Completed in 1896, La Prefectura was the first palace of government in Bolivia. When the government was moved to La Paz, the magnificent structure became the home of the departmental government of Chuquisaca.

La Paz has a population of roughly 800,000, making it the country's third-largest city. Lying 10,650 to 13,250 feet (3,250 to 4,000 m) above

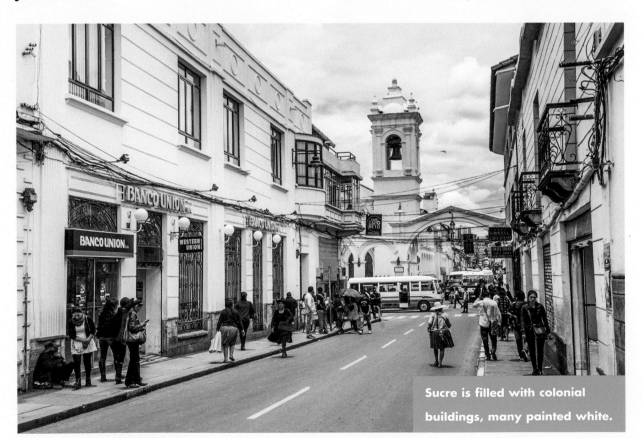

Sucre is filled with colonial buildings, many painted white.

sea level, La Paz is the world's highest national capital. The city was founded in 1548 by the Spanish conquistador Alonso de Mendoza. By the mid-seventeenth century, the city had grown rich through mining and the trade of coca plants. In the wake of the 1952 revolution led by the Nationalist Revolutionary Movement (MNR), many Aymaras of the Altiplano migrated to La Paz, increasing the city's population and making it predominantly Aymara.

La Paz's major industries are food processing and the manufacture of clothing, building materials, tobacco products, chemicals, agricultural tools, and other consumer goods.

Much of La Paz is dominated by modern buildings.

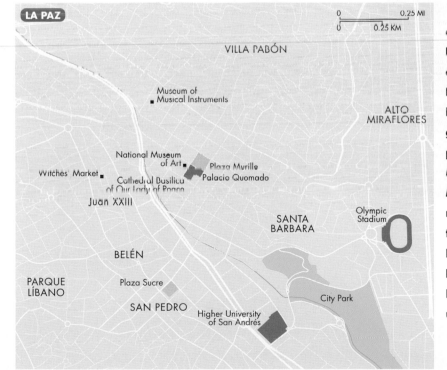

The city is a popular tourist destination, offering visitors many historic buildings and world-class cultural sites and activities. On the Plaza Murillo sits the Cathedral Basilica of Our Lady of Peace, government palaces, and Bolivia's premier art gallery, the National Museum of Art. At the Witches' Market, merchants sell herbal medicines, charms, and ritual items to curious tourists and traditional healers. From Spanish colonial buildings to towering skyscrapers, La Paz blends the old and the new unlike any other city in the country.

The Judicial Branch

The Supreme Court is the highest court in Bolivia. It is made up of seven judges who are elected by popular vote for six-year terms. Judges may not be reelected.

There is one district court in each of Bolivia's nine departments, as well as provincial and local courts to try minor cases.

Bolivia also has several specialized courts. The Constitutional Court rules on the constitutionality of government

A Bolivian woman casts her vote in a presidential election. Voting is required by law in Bolivia.

Evo Morales worked as a farmer and a labor leader before entering politics.

Bolivia's Longtime President

Evo Morales was born In 1959 in Isallavi, a small village in the western highlands. A member of the Aymara ethnic group, Morales was the country's first president to come from the indigenous population. In the mid-1990s, Morales helped found the Movement Toward Socialism (MAS) political party, which supported the government taking over, or nationalizing, some industries.

In 1997, Morales was elected to the Chamber of Deputies, and then in 2006 he became president. Once in office, he instituted programs to reduce poverty and illiteracy, especially among indigenous groups. Morales led the movement that ultimately resulted in a new constitution in 2009. The constitution gave the government tighter control over Bolivia's natural resources and furthered indigenous rights.

Morales won his second and third terms in 2009 and 2014, respectively, but economic conditions in Bolivia had caused increased opposition to his policies. In 2010, violent protests broke out across the country over unemployment and rising fuel prices. The following year, Morales supported a plan to build a highway that would go through Isiboro Sécure National Park and Indigenous Territory.

In 2016, Bolivian voters rejected a proposed change in the constitution that would have allowed Morales to run for reelection a fourth time. Bolivia's courts, however, ruled Morales could run again in 2019.

Supporters of the Movement Toward Socialism attend a rally.

or court actions. The Agrarian and Environmental Tribunal handles matters of agriculture and the environment. The Judiciary Council oversees the conduct of judges and courts.

Voting and Political Parties

All Bolivian citizens over the age of eighteen must vote. Individuals who do not vote may be denied access to their bank accounts. Another penalty imposed on nonvoters is having their passports or government identification cards seized. Compulsory voting rules are often not enforced among senior citizens.

Bolivia has a multiparty system. From 1982 to 2005, three parties dominated Bolivian politics. They were the Nationalist Revolutionary Movement, the Revolutionary Left Movement, and the Nationalist Democratic Action. Because no one party was able to maintain power alone, the parties agreed to work together to form coalition governments.

Since 2006, the political party called the Movement Toward Socialism (MAS) has governed the country, with Evo Morales serving as president. The MAS is firmly in control of the Bolivian legislature, holding a majority of seats in both houses. Members of the National Unity Front and the Christian Democratic Party hold the remainder of the seats.

Regional Government

Bolivia is divided into nine departments, which are similar to states. Each department is run by a governor, who serves as political, military, and administrative authority in the department. Each department is divided into regions called provinces. Within these are municipalities, which are like counties. Mayors and municipal councils govern the municipalities.

DEPARTMENTS

Pando

El Beni

La Paz

Cochabamba

Santa Cruz

Oruro

Potosí

Chuquisaca

Tarija

CHAPTER 6

Vast Potential

Opposite: **A cowboy herds cattle in eastern Bolivia. Beef is the most popular meat in the country.**

BOLIVIA HAS BEEN EXPERIENCING GREAT ECONOMIC growth in recent times. Between 2004 and 2014, the Brazilian economy experienced an average growth rate of a healthy 5 percent each year. Increased exports of natural gas to Argentina were the main reason for the country's consistent economic expansion throughout the decade.

Despite the good news, Bolivia remains one of the poorest countries in South America. Although an average of just 4 percent of Bolivians were unemployed in recent years, 39 percent of Bolivians live in poverty. Nearly 60 percent of Bolivian families live in areas that lack basic services, such as fresh running water and sanitation. Nearly 70 percent of Bolivian houses have dirt floors.

Though rich in natural resources, Bolivia faces many challenges as it attempts to achieve economic prosperity. One

Llamas cross a road in the Altiplano.

reason is the country's geography. Poor roads and no direct access to the sea make it difficult to transport and ship products. Government restrictions on foreign investment have also hindered Bolivia's economic development. The quality of education is poor, especially in rural areas, where nearly 80 percent of the population lives in poverty. For the young, a lack of education limits their future employment outlook.

Oil and Gas

Bolivia's economic future is dependent on the country's oil and natural gas reserves. These resources are located primarily in the eastern lowlands. The nation's oil fields produce about 60,000 barrels of crude oil a day.

Bolivia's oil fields were first developed by the Standard Oil Company of New Jersey, an American company. In 1937, after the Chaco War between Bolivia and Paraguay, the Bolivian government took over the oil fields. The oil industry was controlled by the state until 1952. At that time, the government began accepting foreign investment to further exploit the nation's oil reserves.

In 2006, President Evo Morales announced that a majority of oil and gas production would be Bolivian owned. Most Bolivians supported his decree. Since then, foreign companies have left Bolivia and stopped oil exploration. State control of the industry has resulted in much greater revenues for the Bolivian government. From 2006 to 2016, the move generated $31.5 billion for the government.

An oil refinery in Cochabamba. In 2016, Bolivia produced 58,000 barrels of oil per day.

Bolivia has the second-largest natural gas reserves in South America, after Venezuela. About 80 percent of the reserves are found in the Tarija Department in the east. The country produces an average of 58 million cubic meters of gas per day, with about half going to Brazil and one-quarter going to Argentina. The gas is exported via pipeline to both countries.

Oil and natural gas exports account for about 55 percent of Bolivia's total exports and about 14 percent of the country's gross domestic product (GDP), the total value of goods produced and services provided in a country. Natural gas makes up most of these revenues.

Workers push a cart at a mine in Potosí. Once the world's largest silver producer, Potosí is now a major supplier of zinc and tin.

Mining

For nearly three centuries, silver was the economic backbone of Spain's colonial government in Bolivia. When the price of silver began to decline in the 1870s, Bolivians began to look for a new metal to replace silver. In the early 1900s, worldwide demand for tin soared, and tin prices reached historic highs. In 1900, Bolivia supplied 12 percent of the world's supply of tin. By 1910, it supplied 20 percent. By 1945, Bolivian tin production reached its peak, at 49 percent of the world's total production. Today, Bolivia is the world's fourth-largest producer of tin.

Important metals and minerals mined in Bolivia include zinc, lead, copper, tungsten, antimony, sulfur, lithium, potassium, and borax. Gold and silver are also mined. It is estimated that only 10 percent of Bolivia's mineral resources have been tapped.

Agriculture

The agriculture industry employs about 40 percent of Bolivians and contributes 13 percent to the country's GDP. Yet only about 4 percent of the land in Bolivia is arable, or able to be farmed. About two-thirds of Bolivia's farmers live in the Altiplano. Earning a living as a farmer is difficult in the dry, cold conditions of these highlands. Most farmers have small plots of land they work with traditional methods. Oxen and horses are used to plow the land. Potatoes, beans, corn, and quinoa are the most commonly grown crops. Sheep, llamas, and alpacas are the most common livestock. Their food, milk, wool, and hides provide many of a family's needs.

The warm, fertile valleys of the Yungas are home to about 20 percent of the nation's farmers. These regions grow corn, bananas, oranges, carrots, onions, beets, and cabbage. In the higher altitudes, coffee, cacao, wheat, rye, oats, and coca are grown.

The rich soils of the eastern lowlands provide ideal growing conditions for sugarcane, fruit, soybeans, sunflowers, and

A worker separates quinoa seeds from other material on a farm in the Altiplano. Bolivia is the world's second-largest producer of quinoa.

Some boliviano coins are made from two different metals.

Money Facts

The boliviano is the basic unit of Bolivian currency. It is divided into 100 centavos. In 2018, 1 boliviano equaled 14¢, and 6.93 bolivianos equaled $1. Coins are in values of 5, 10, 20, and 50 centavos, and 1, 2, and 5 bolivianos. The front of the coins contain the coin's value, the date of issue, and the phrase *La Union Es La Fuerza* (The Union Is Strength). The reverse side features the Bolivian coat of arms, which contains an image of Cerro Rico, where silver was discovered in 1544.

Banknotes, or paper money, come in values of 10, 20, 50, 100, and 200 bolivianos. The banknotes were redesigned in 2018 to reflect the nation's multicultural heritage.

cotton. The Santa Cruz and El Beni departments are home to Bolivia's largest cattle ranches.

Manufacturing

Manufacturing accounts for about 13 percent of Bolivia's GDP. The sector has grown in recent decades, but remains mostly

A worker packs sugar into bags at a plant in central Bolivia.

limited to small or midsized factories. Food processing is the largest segment of the manufacturing industry. Activities include making dairy products, distilling alcohol, and refining and processing sugarcane and sugar beets. Cochabamba is noted for its fruit and vegetable processing facilities. Santa Cruz is the home of soybean processing plants.

The manufacturing industry also produces plastics, fertilizers, paint, chemicals, and medicines. Smelters refine minerals such as lead, tin, and zinc. The construction industry produces cement and other materials used in building, including clay and salt. Metal industries produce a range of consumer goods, including batteries, vehicles, farm equipment, and appliances.

Bolivia has extensive timber resources. Tropical forests cover roughly half of Bolivia's land area. The timber industry is strong in the lowlands. Flat, sawed wood is the country's main wood product. Most of it is exported to Brazil. Timber also supports the country's paper industry. A small number of companies produce newsprint, cardboard, and paper goods.

What Bolivia Grows, Makes, and Mines

Agriculture

Potatoes (2014)	1,069,010 metric tons
Corn (2018)	875,000 metric tons
Cattle (2015)	8,847,434 animals

Manufacturing (2016, value of exports)

Soybean products	$960,000,000
Alcohol	$51,800,000
Wood products	$46,700,000

Mining (2016)

Natural Gas	21.1 billion cubic meters
Oil	58,077 barrels per day
Tin	18,000 metric tons

Service Industries

The service industry—businesses that provide work and products to customers, but are not involved in manufacturing—accounts for 54 percent of Bolivia's GDP. Nearly half of Bolivia's population works in service industries such as health care, banking and finance, and retail sales. Many people work in Bolivia's government as teachers, law enforcement personnel, and administrators.

Bolivia's tourist industry is increasing. The country's natural beauty and historic cities and ruins attract tourists from around the world. In recent years, the number of visitors to Bolivia has more than doubled. In 2016, 1.2 million tourists traveled to Bolivia. The travel and tourist industry accounts for about 7 percent of Bolivia's GDP. Roughly 320,000 people work in tourism and tourism-related jobs.

Many tourists who travel to Bolivia enjoy strolling the narrow colonial streets.

Transportation

Travel within Bolivia is sometimes difficult. The rugged geography in some areas makes the building of roads and railroads a

Mi Teleférico

Bolivian officials have begun to introduce an innovative means of travel *above* the nation's cities. In 2014, Mi Teleférico (My Cable Car), a spectacular cable car system, was opened between La Paz and El Alto. The overhead car system spanned more than 6 miles (10 km) at 1,300 feet (396 m)—the longest urban cable car system in the world. Since that time, the system has been expanded to nearly 11 miles (18 km). Each day, around 100,000 passengers use the system to travel between the two cities. Users prefer the quick, comfortable teleférico system to the crowded vans and buses that run on the streets below. The *New York Times* called Bolivia's solution to urban travel a "subway in the sky." When completed, the entire system will run 21 miles (34 km) with 11 lines and 39 stations.

daunting challenge. The Andes limits movement in the west. In the lowlands, heavy rains and floods often wash out roads.

Of Bolivia's 56,276 miles (90,567 km) of road, only 6,084 miles (9,791 km) are paved. The remaining roads are gravel or dirt. The 30,000-mile (48,000 km) Pan-American Highway, which stretches from Alaska to the tip of Argentina, runs along the western spine of South America. A spur of the highway leads into Bolivia. As the country's capital, La Paz is the hub of all road transportation. Paved roads connect the capital to the Peruvian border, the port of Arica in northern Chile, Potosí, Cochabamba, and Santa Cruz.

Railways run for 2,177 miles (3,504 km), divided into two segments. The western segment connects La Paz to the Chilean ports, the port of Guaqui on Lake Titicaca, and cities in the Altiplano and Andean valleys. However, maintenance of the western segment is poor, and many portions are closed. The eastern segment links Brazil to Argentina.

A small ferry carries a bus across the waters of Lake Titicaca. It is the world's highest navigable lake.

The narrow Yungas Road is cut into mountainsides.

The Most Dangerous Road in the World

One of the few routes that connects the Yungas region to the capital city of La Paz has been called the "world's most dangerous road." The Yungas Road was carved into the side of the Cordillera Oriental mountain range in the 1930s. Many sections of the 43-mile-long (69 km) road were single-lane and unpaved. There were few guardrails to prevent cars from tumbling into the valleys below—a drop of 15,260 feet (4,650 m) in some spots. Mudslides, falling rocks, high winds, and fog made the drive even more dangerous. An estimated two to three hundred people were killed on the Yungas Road each year, until 2006 when improvements were made. Though the new road is considerably safer, thrill-seeking mountain bikers and careless drivers continue to lose their lives on Bolivia's "Death Road."

Air transportation is important because of the country's difficult ground travel. Bolivia has 855 airports, but only 21 have paved runways. Bolivia's principal airports are El Alto International in La Paz and Viru Viru International in Santa Cruz. Bolivia's national airline, Boliviana de Aviación, or BoA, began operations in 2009. The airline serves cities in Bolivia and a limited number of foreign destinations.

CHAPTER 7

People and Language

WITH 11.2 MILLION PEOPLE, BOLIVIA HAS THE eighth-largest population among the thirteen South American countries. The country covers a relatively large amount of land, however. As a result, it has the lowest population density in South America, just 26 people per square mile (10 per sq km).

Bolivia's population is unequally distributed. Most Bolivians live in the fertile valleys and hillsides of the highlands. The Amazon basin, plains, and the southeastern Chaco are far less inhabited.

The population of Bolivia is relatively young. About 32 percent of Bolivia's population is under fifteen years of age, whereas the average for all South American countries is 24 percent. Life expectancy in Bolivia averages sixty-nine years, the lowest in South America, where the average is seventy-five years.

Opposite: **A Bolivian woman carrying her baby.**

PERU

BRAZIL

La Paz
El Alto
Cochabamba
Oruro
Santa Cruz

Sucre

PARAGUAY

CHILE

ARGENTINA

Population of Major Cities (2012)

Santa Cruz	1,453,549
El Alto	848,840
La Paz	764,617
Cochabamba	630,587
Oruro	264,683

On the Move

The most significant population change in Bolivia in recent times is the rapid growth of cities. People leave rural areas to find jobs and gain access to better education and health care for their children. Between 1950 and 2012, Bolivia's urban population grew at an average annual rate of nearly 4 percent. In 1990, about 50 percent of the population lived in cities. By 2018, 69 percent lived in urban areas.

No city in Bolivia has experienced such large-scale migration as El Alto. In the 1980s, El Alto was a small suburb of La Paz. Since then, hundreds of thousands of people from the rural areas have poured into the city. Many people in El Alto live in deep poverty. They live in shacks made of plywood or tin, without running water, electricity, or sewer services.

In response, neighborhood committees operate in the city to improve the quality of life for people in El Alto's poorest areas. These local groups determine the residents' needs for electricity, safe drinking water, telephone service, employment, and other services and present them to government officials. Recent state projects to improve conditions in El Alto have been effective in many poorer neighborhoods.

Ethnicity

Roughly 20 percent of Bolivians refer to themselves as indigenous. They are the descendants of the original people who inhabited Bolivia. About 70 percent of Bolivians are mestizos, people with a mixture of indigenous and European background. People of solely European background make up about 5 percent of the population. Bolivians of African descent account for about 1 percent of the population. There are also small numbers of Bolivians of Asian descent.

Many Bolivians are leaving the countryside for the city. El Alto has grown quickly, with red brick buildings spreading over hillsides.

Mestizos

Most mestizos have a mixed indigenous and Spanish background, but there are small groups of people of German, Italian, Turkish, Lebanese, and Croatian descent. Geographically, mestizos are more widely distributed than any other ethnic group in Bolivia. Today, large numbers of mestizos make their home in Santa Cruz, Cochabamba, and the Yungas.

Most mestizos speak and write Spanish, although many can also speak an indigenous language. During the colonial period, mestizos comprised the majority group in regions

Bolivians of Italian descent prepare Italian food in Cochabamba.

Common Spanish Words and Phrases

Spanish	English
Hola	Hello
Buenos días	Good morning
Buenas tardes	Good evening
¿Cómo estás?	How are you?
Gracias	Thank you
De nada	You're welcome
¿Cómo te llamas?	What is your name?
¿Cuánto?	How much?
¿Dónde está . . . ?	Where is . . . ?
¿Qué es esto?	What is this?
¿Hablas inglés?	Do you speak English?
Me llamo . . .	My name is . . .
Sí	Yes
¡Felicitaciones!	Congratulations!
¡Feliz cumpleaños!	Happy birthday!

where Spanish was spoken. They held more rights and privileges than other minority groups in the country but fewer than the European-born whites.

Traditionally, mestizos worked as clerks and small-scale businesspeople. Today, mestizos are well established in professions such as medicine, law, industry, technology, and the arts.

Aymara and Quechua

Bolivia has the largest percentage of indigenous people of any country in South America. Most live in the highlands, where they farm. There, they maintain their culture and identity. Most speak Spanish as well as an indigenous language. The two major indigenous groups in Bolivia are the Aymara and the Quechua.

The Aymara people originated in what is now central Peru. Strong-willed and independent, the Aymaras retained their language and customs after first being conquered by the Incas and later by the Spanish.

Traditionally, Aymaras live in small communities and compounds called *ayllu*, made up of several extended families.

Aymara festivals often feature elaborate masks.

Know Your Numbers

English	Spanish	Quechua	Aymara
One	Uno	Huk	Maya
Two	Dos	Iskay	Paya
Three	Tres	Kinsa	Quimsa
Four	Cuatro	Tawa	Pusi
Five	Cinco	Pisqa	Phiska
Six	Seis	Suqta	Sojjta
Seven	Siete	Qanchis	Pakalko
Eight	Ocho	Pusaq	Quimsakalko
Nine	Nueve	Isqun	Yatunka
Ten	Diez	Chunka	Tunka

A typical Aymara house is made of mud bricks with roofs of rough thatch or corrugated metal. The Aymara people grow carrots, potatoes, corn, and onions on small plots of land. For centuries, Aymaras have grown and chewed coca plants. They also use the plant in traditional medicine and religious rituals.

The Aymara language is one of Bolivia's three official languages, the others being Spanish and Quechua. Nearly three million people in Bolivia, Argentina, Peru, and Chile speak Aymara. More than half of them live in Bolivia. Depending upon region, different dialects, or versions, of Aymara are spoken. The dialects are closely related, however, and are all mutually understandable.

The Quechua people trace their roots to the Incan Empire. Modern Quechuas are more widespread geographically than Aymaras, but are settled primarily in the high Andes and the departments of Cochabamba and Chuquisaca. Like Aymaras, most Quechuas live in farming communities in similar types

A Mosetén woman makes a basket from reeds. The Mosetén are among Bolivia's many different indigenous ethnic groups.

of housing. Potatoes, quinoa, and corn are the main crops grown by Quechua people. Their livestock includes llamas and sheep, whose wool is used to weave warm clothing.

Quechua is the most widely spoken indigenous language in Bolivia. Roughly 4.5 million people speak the language in Bolivia, Peru, Ecuador, Chile, Argentina, and Brazil. Some Quechua dialects differ vastly from others, making mutual understanding impossible. Words spoken in English that originated in the Quechua language include *condor* (*kuntur* in Quechua), *jerky* (*ch'arki*), and *quinine* (*kina*).

Other Indigenous Groups

The eastern shores of Lake Titicaca, north of La Paz, are home to the Kallawaya people. They may be descendants of the Tiwanaku culture. The Kallawaya people are known as traveling healers with a deep understanding about the medicinal properties of plants, minerals, and animals. They travel throughout northeastern Bolivia and parts of neighboring countries to treat patients. Kallawayas speak both the Kallawaya and Quechua languages.

The Chipaya people also trace their origins to the Tiwanaku civilization. They live in and around the remote town of Santa Ana de Chipaya on the edge of the Coipasa salt desert. The town is made up of round mud brick houses with corrugated

The Chipaya people of the Altiplano have traditionally lived in round houses made of mud bricks with thatched roofs.

Quechua
Cavineña
Movima
Aymara
Trinitario
Guarayu
Aymara
Quechua
Chiquitano
Chipaya
Ayoreo
Chiquitano
Aymara
Quechua
Guarani
Quechua

KEY
Aymara Native group

iron or thatched roofs, a church, and a cemetery. On the nearby plain, Chipayas grow quinoa and herd llamas and sheep. Barely able to scratch out a living, many Chipaya people move to Bolivian cities to find work. Others cross the border to work in Chilean mines.

Other Ethnic Groups

Bolivians of African heritage are the descendants of people who were brought to South America to work in mines and were enslaved. Most black Bolivians live in the Yungas, but communities exist in all major Bolivian cities. Black Bolivians speak mostly Spanish, and those living in the Yungas speak Aymara as well. Because of racism, black Bolivians have a difficult time finding steady jobs in cities such as La Paz. Women often work as household servants, while men may find employment in small shops or as drivers.

Bolivia is also home to some people of Japanese heritage. Some are the descendants of people who arrived in Bolivia in the late 1800s to work on plantations. Many more arrived in the 1950s to farm the eastern parts of the country. The Japanese government helped establish two communities, Okinawa and San Juan de Yapacaní. Today, many people in these communities continue to speak Japanese in addition to Spanish.

Bolivia's Mennonites drive horse-drawn carriages. They live a traditional life without modern conveniences.

A World Apart

The Mennonites are a religious group that originated in northern Europe. Many Mennonites choose to live in a traditional way. They work as farmers, without electricity or automobiles. The Mennonites have migrated frequently over the centuries in search of religious freedom and to try to separate themselves from the modern world.

Several dozen Mennonite families arrived in Bolivia in the 1950s. Over the years, others came and families grew. Today, there are roughly sixty Mennonite colonies in Bolivia totaling about seventy thousand people. The Mennonites of Bolivia speak a dialect of German.

CHAPTER 8

The Faiths of a People

RELIGION PLAYS A CENTRAL ROLE IN MODERN Bolivian life and is guided by three main themes: the Catholic Church; the ancient rites and traditional religious beliefs practiced by indigenous Bolivians; and the rise of Evangelical Protestant churches.

Roman Catholicism

Seventy-seven percent of Bolivians are Roman Catholic. Many people, however, practice traditional indigenous rites along with Catholicism.

Spaniards introduced the Roman Catholic religion to Bolivia when they conquered the region in the sixteenth century. Catholicism became the state religion during the Spanish colonial period and remained the official religion of Bolivia until 2009. The country's 2009 constitution

Opposite: **Religion in Bolivia is often syncretic, a blend of different beliefs. One of the largest festivals in La Paz is El Gran Poder. The dancers at the festival exhibit devotion that mixes Catholicism and traditional indigenous beliefs.**

Religion in Bolivia	
Roman Catholic	77%
Protestant	16%
Other	2%
None	5%

Catholics attend Mass in Santa Cruz.

established Bolivia as a secular state, "independent of religion." The constitution proclaims, "The State respects and guarantees freedom of religion and spiritual beliefs, according to each individual's view of the world."

Missionaries from a religious group called the Jesuit order were responsible for the spread of Catholicism in Bolivia's lowlands. Arriving from Paraguay, the Jesuits established several missions in Chiquitos, a province in the modern-day Department of Santa Cruz. The missions were well-organized communities with churches, workshops, schools, and

cemeteries. The compounds also included housing for the people the Jesuits converted to Christianity.

Protestants

Protestants account for 16 percent of the Bolivian religious community. Half belong to evangelical denominations, which focus on the authority of the Bible and an emotional connection to God. Evangelical denominations are the fastest-growing religious groups in the country. The rapid growth of evangelicalism in Bolivia reflects a similar trend that has taken place throughout Latin America. The population of Latin American Protestants has grown from fifty thousand in 1900 to more than sixty-four million in 2015. Evangelical and Pentecostal churches make up roughly three-quarters of this growth.

Many of the country's evangelical churches are established by religious organizations based in the United States, Europe, or other parts of Latin America. These include Evangelical

The Customs of Copacabana

The Basilica of Our Lady of Copacabana is one of Bolivia's most sacred sites. The glistening white cathedral overlooks the southeastern shore of Lake Titicaca. Construction of the basilica began in 1668 and was completed in 1805.

Inside the cathedral stands a statue of the Most Blessed Virgin of the Candelaria, Our Lady of Copacabana. Francisco Tito Yupanqui carved the statue in 1583. The wooden statue wears a flowing white robe and is crowned with a golden halo. It stands in a glass-enclosed case made of gold and silver. The statue is never removed: Worshippers believe this could cause deadly floods.

During the week leading up to Easter, thousands of Bolivians make a pilgrimage to the basilica for a blessing from the Lady of Copacabana. Some come from as far away as Santa Cruz or Potosí. While many people drive to the city, others make the journey on foot. From La Paz, pilgrims walk nearly 100 miles (160 km) to reach Copacabana.

Pilgrims pray before the statue of the Virgin at Copacabana.

Methodists and Pentecostals. Other Protestants present in Bolivia include Lutherans and Anglicans.

Traditional Religions

Many indigenous Bolivians practice Catholicism while also continuing to honor traditional beliefs and customs. An

Aymara or Quechua person, for example, may pray to Catholic saints, while also offering sacrifices to Pachamama, the goddess Mother Earth. According to traditional Aymara belief, humankind was created from the land. Because earth is considered the mother of humankind, many people pray and make offerings to Pachamama in a ritual called *ch'alla*. Coca leaves and other gifts are offered when people pray for good health, a plentiful harvest, and the safety of the family. A ch'alla ceremony can be conducted by a Catholic priest or a *yatiri*, an Aymara spiritual leader.

Some of Bolivia's ethnic groups are animist. Animism is the religious belief that all things have a spirit or soul. These groups worship animals, mountains, the sun, the moon, and other objects. The spirit of a deceased ancestor or other

Bolivians pray at an evangelical church in La Paz.

important person might inhabit any of these, so to show respect for ancestors, worshippers give offerings to such objects.

Day of the Dead

One of the most important dates in the religious calendar of native Bolivians is November 2, Day of the Dead. Also known as All Saints' Day, the holiday is an example of how the traditional beliefs of indigenous cultures are mixed with the practices of Catholicism.

The Aymara people believe the spirits of the dead visit their relatives at this time of the year. The spirits, however, must be fed for their journey back to the afterlife. On November 2, Bolivians visit the cemeteries of their relatives and decorate the graves with flowers. They also spread out large meals for the deceased, which include cake, candy, and fruits. Some people leave behind small dolls made of bread that represent the family members who have died. Breads in the shape of ladders and horses are offered to help the spirits return to heaven.

A shaman, a person who uses ritual to communicate with spirits or tell the future, makes an offering to Pachamama.

Musicians also play a part in the day's activities. Solo performers and bands play folk songs to wish the spirits a happy journey home.

The Day of the Dead is a national holiday in Bolivia. Most businesses are shut down. Much work is done to prepare for the event. In the days leading up to the holiday, the government hires workmen to repair damaged graves. Families clean headstones and prepare gifts of food. For the living, the Day of the Dead is a welcome opportunity to reunite with respected ancestors.

Many Bolivians bring bread figures to the graves of their loved ones on the Day of the Dead.

CHAPTER 9

A Rich Culture

THE CULTURE OF BOLIVIA IS A RICH MIX OF INDIGENOUS traditions, Spanish traditions, and other influences. Bolivians express their joy of life through art, music, architecture, dance, and clothing. President Evo Morales has called on Bolivians to celebrate the indigenous cultures of their nation. Morales, Bolivia's first president to come from the indigenous population, hopes to spread Bolivian traditions among all people. "We have an unimaginable cultural wealth and we would like it to be recognized all over the world," he said.

Opposite: **Bolivians perform a traditional dance at a festival in Copacabana on the shores of Lake Titicaca.**

Music

Because of Bolivia's ethnic mix, traditional Bolivian music varies greatly from region to region. The music of the Andes and the Altiplano is slow, haunting, and sad. Traditional Andean music is played on flutes, guitars, and reed pipes called

Solitude

Adela Zamudio was a Bolivian poet and educator. Born in 1854 in Cochabamba, she is considered the country's greatest poet, but she did not write under her own name. Instead she used the pen name Soledad, meaning "Solitude." She did this to show the isolation she felt as a woman working in Bolivia.

Zamudio's poetry dealt with social issues, such as the inequalities between men and women. Zamudio was an outspoken pioneer for women's rights, supporting women's labor movements and fair divorce laws. Her most famous short poem, "Nacer Hombre" (To Be Born a Man), was published in 1887. At the time, women did not have the right to vote in Bolivia.

A smart, classy woman
Can't vote in elections,
But the poorest felon can.
(Pardon my surprise.)
If he can just sign his name
Even an idiot can vote
Because he's a man!

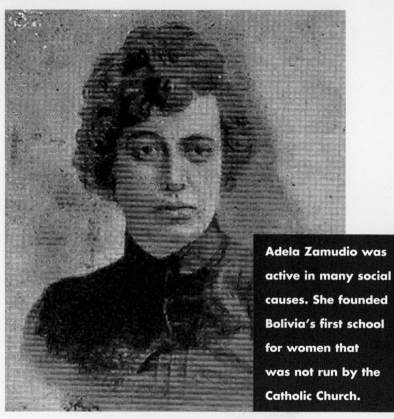

Adela Zamudio was active in many social causes. She founded Bolivia's first school for women that was not run by the Catholic Church.

Zamudio composed many of her poems in the Quechua language. As an educator, she created a spelling book in Quechua that was used in schools. Her birthday, October 11, is celebrated as Bolivian Women's Day.

zampoñas. For centuries, Quechua and Aymara musicians have played the *charango*, a tiny ten-string guitar. Traditionally, charangos were made from the shells of armadillos. Today they are constructed from hardwood.

Music in the lowlands is fast and festive. Many styles of lowlands music combine indigenous and Spanish elements. The *chacarera* style of music is a blend of Spanish flamenco and Argentine influences. It is usually performed with guitar, violin, and *bombo*, a drum made from a hollowed tree trunk and covered with animal skins. *Taquirari* music is found in the northeast. It too is played on flutes, charangos, and handheld drums, such as the *caja*, a box-shaped percussion instrument.

The music of Tarija in southern Bolivia is the most joyous and the liveliest music in the country. *Zapateo* ("shoe-tapping")

Musicians play flutes at a festival in Potosí.

Jaime Laredo has been a
world-class musician and
conductor for more than
half a century.

music is played to accompany a fast jig-like dance. *Cueca* and
rueda chapaca are styles of festive folk dances played with guitars and violins to accompany colorfully dressed dancers.

Bolivia's most famous performer of classical music is Jaime
Laredo. Born in Cochabamba, Laredo is a master violinist
who serves as the music director of the Vermont Symphony
Orchestra in the United States. He took up violin at the age
of five and made his orchestral debut with the San Francisco
Symphony at age eleven. He has performed with world-class
musicians, and has performed with and conducted orchestras
in major cities throughout Europe and North America.

Modern Bolivian music features popular influences,
including rock, rap, and techno dance music. Atajo has been

The Museum of Musical Instruments

Located on a quaint, cobblestone street in La Paz, the Museum of Musical Instruments is one of the capital's most popular attractions. Ernesto Cavour Aramayo, a Bolivian instrument maker, founded the museum in 1962. The museum features Bolivia's largest collection of indigenous instruments—more than two thousand string, percussion, and wind instruments used in different regions of the country. Many of the charango guitars on display are made from unusual materials, such as armadillo and tortoise shells, mule teeth, and bird beaks. Other unique musical instruments at the museum include flutes made from volcanic rock and rattles made of goat feet. The museum allows visitors to touch and play many of the instruments and take charango lessons in its music classroom.

The bombo, a type of traditional Bolivian drum, has a goat-hair head.

Bolivia's premier rock band since the late 1990s. Many of the group's songs feature political and social messages. Atajo's sounds incorporate reggae, blues, Bolivian folk, and African influences. Bolivia is home to many indigenous rap groups, particularly in the slum neighborhoods of El Alto, outside La Paz. The music is hard and fast, and the lyrics often reflect the struggles of the indigenous people. The music is frequently sung in Aymara rather than Spanish.

Art

The people of the Tiwanaku and Inca cultures were exceptional artists and craftspeople. Tiwanaku pottery, including bowls, jars, and cups, were created with orange-colored clay.

Baroque in Bolivia

Baroque was the preeminent form of European music in the 1600s and early 1700s, the time when missionaries were arriving in Bolivia. The missionaries brought baroque music with them and taught indigenous people to play European instruments. Together, the missionaries and indigenous people wrote baroque music.

This unusual musical legacy has endured.

Today, many people in eastern Bolivia play harps, violins, and lutes, enjoying the music of a distant time. Every two years, a huge festival of baroque music in the Jesuit Missions of Chiquitos honors this tradition. Top musicians come from all over Latin America and Europe to play dozens of concerts in what has become one of South America's largest musical events.

Most are brightly painted with designs of animals and geometric shapes. Many vessels were created in the shape of human heads as depictions of a real person. The Incas produced magnificent work in silver, gold, ceramics, and textiles.

During the colonial period, European influences were

introduced into Bolivian art. Religious subjects and portraits of wealthy people were common. The leading mestizo artist of the period was Melchor Pérez de Holguín. He was active mainly in Potosí, the silver-rich cultural center of South America. Pérez de Holguín mixed European influences with indigenous styles to create a unique art form. Many of his paintings feature Catholic saints and political events. Some of Pérez de Holguín's religious paintings can be found in Potosí's churches and convents.

Many fine Bolivian artists earned prominence in the twentieth century. Cecilio Guzmán de Rojas painted Aymara subjects, such as portraits of people and beautiful landscapes of the

Cecilio Guzmán de Rojas focused on Bolivian subjects in his art, such as this portrait of an indigenous woman.

A Rich Culture **113**

Girls play soccer in Potosí. The sport is growing in popularity among young women.

highlands. Guzmán de Rojas also created a series of drawings showing the suffering of soldiers during the Chaco War. Other acclaimed Bolivian painters include Graciela Rodo Boulanger, María Luisa Pacheco, and Arturo Borda.

Marina Núñez del Prado was one of Latin America's most renowned sculptors. Working in wood, granite, marble, onyx, and basalt, her works combined grace and power. Del Prado spent the last twenty-five years of her life working in Lima, Peru. The National Museum of Nuñez del Prado, her family home in Lima, houses more than a thousand pieces of her work, including drawings, sculptures, and sketches.

Sports

Soccer, or *fútbol*, is Bolivia's most beloved sport. The game is played in rural yards, city streets, school playgrounds, and huge stadiums. From the time a child is old enough to walk, he or she is playing soccer.

 Enchantment of the World Bolivia

The Bolivia national soccer team, called La Verde (The Green) or Los Altiplanos (The Highlanders), has played in international competitions since 1926. La Verde's greatest victory came in 1963. That year, Bolivia hosted and won the South American Championship title, the continent's most important soccer tournament.

Bolivians enjoy a variety of other sports and recreational activities, including basketball, volleyball, horseback riding, mountain climbing, swimming, and hiking. Mountain biking and motorbike racing are also popular.

Boys ride bikes in the Altiplano.

CHAPTER 10

Daily Life

DESPITE THEIR CULTURAL AND REGIONAL DIFFER-ences, Bolivians have much in common with their fellow countrymen. Bolivians tend to display values such as politeness and courtesy. The elderly and people in positions of authority are generally treated with respect and are highly regarded for their place in society. Cheerful and pleasant to strangers, Bolivians are generous and appreciate people who are warm and friendly.

Opposite: **An elderly Bolivian woman in Potosí. Women in Bolivia have a life expectancy of seventy-two, whereas men can expect to live sixty-seven years.**

Education

According to Bolivian law, children must attend school from the ages of six to fourteen. The law, however, is not regularly enforced. Though schools exist in nearly all areas of the country, the government does not provide enough funds to improve schools and hire quality teachers. The quality of education in rural areas is lower than in cities. Children in rural regions frequently miss days or drop out of school entirely to help work on the family farm. Many schools in rural areas are difficult to travel to or are in poor condition. Rural students often do not advance beyond the second or third grade.

Many wealthier families send their children to private schools and institutes. Many of the schools are run by churches. Private schools are especially popular in cities, including among middle-class and lower middle–class

Most schools in Bolivia require uniforms.

families. At least half of the students in cities attend a private school. International schools in Bolivia include American and British schools that teach in English, and high-quality Spanish, Japanese, and French schools.

Secondary education, or high school, is available for fourteen- to seventeen-year-old students. Few secondary schools are located in rural areas.

Higher education includes different specialized schools, such as trade and business schools, as well as universities. One of the most popular universities in Bolivia is the University of Saint Francis Xavier in Sucre. The institution is known for its excellent programs in agriculture, engineering, and education. Other respected institutions include the Higher University of San Andrés in La Paz and Nur University in Santa Cruz.

The University of Saint Francis Xavier in Sucre is the second-oldest university in the Western Hemisphere. It was founded in 1624.

Health Care

Under the administration of President Evo Morales, health care in Bolivia has improved. Bolivians are entitled to medical treatment under the National Health Fund, which often offers free medical care for a variety of ailments. Most cities and large rural areas have access to facilities that provide basic services. Western medicine in more remote areas is not available. People in the countryside often use traditional medicines. A shortage of hospitals, clinics, doctors, and nurses further strains Bolivia's health care system.

An Aymara healer performs a ceremony for a family in Copacabana.

Child's Play

One of the most popular children's games in Bolivia is *trompo*. The game is played with wooden tops that have a metal point. A circle is drawn on the ground with chalk and two or more players spin their tops inside the circle. As the tops spin, each player hopes his or her top bumps into the other tops to either knock them out of the circle or make them stop spinning. The winner is the player with the last top spinning in the circle.

The country's infant mortality rate—the death of an infant before his or her first birthday—is thirty-five deaths per one thousand births, in comparison to ten deaths in nearby Argentina, six in the United States, and two in Japan. Bolivia's infant mortality rate is the highest in South America. Children living in rural regions have significantly higher mortality rates than those in urban areas.

Poverty and the lack of adequate health care in Bolivia put many people at risk of dangerous diseases, including hepatitis, typhoid fever, and tuberculosis. Measles and diarrhea cause many infant deaths. Roughly 15 percent of children under five years old suffer from malnutrition. Bolivians living in many rural areas and poor communities in large cities lack safe water and proper sanitation services. The absence of these basic services contributes to the spread of illness and disease.

Chullo hats keep Bolivians warm in the cold mountains.

Clothing

The kind of clothes people wear in Bolivia often depends on their ethnicity. Many indigenous men wear light cotton trousers, which are usually homemade. The pants are often accompanied by a colorful pancho and a woolen cap called a *chullo*. Most men in Bolivia, however, now dress in Western-style clothing, such as jeans, jackets, and T-shirts.

Indigenous women often maintain their traditional style of fashion. Highland Indian

Marriage, Bolivian Style

For a couple to be legally married in Bolivia, their wedding ceremony must be performed by a justice of the peace. Many couples also have a second religious ceremony, usually in a Catholic church. Among the Aymara, the ceremony is followed by a joyous reception where the guests make offerings of beer to Pachamama, Mother Earth. Guests perform this ritual by pouring a portion of their first beer into a crate that contains bottles of beer. The ritual is believed to bring good health and good luck to the newlyweds. Household appliances are commonly given as gifts to the new couple. Sometimes gifts of cash are pinned onto the groom's suit.

women wear long skirts called *polleras*. These brightly colored skirts are worn tight at the waist and flare outward below the knee. Polleras are made of several layers, each pleated and each equally colorful. With the pollera, women wear a colorful shawl called a *manta*, and a frilly blouse. Earrings or pendants are commonly worn, particularly during special occasions such as festivals or parades.

Women in the lowlands and the Chaco might wear a *tipoi*, a sleeveless, tunic-like dress that reaches to the ankles. The dresses are often adorned with colorful ribbons. Depending on the region, tipois can be bell-shaped or more tubular and fitted.

Headwear provides a crowning touch to the indigenous Bolivian woman's wardrobe. Hats come in many different shapes and are usually dark colored. The most popular type of hat is the *bombín*, or bowler. The hat is worn to show the marital status of the woman. If the hat is worn perched on the side, the woman is single or widowed. If it is worn straight and on top of the head, the woman is married.

In Bolivia, potatoes come in many shapes and colors.

Food

Bolivian dishes are often a mixture of Spanish cuisine and traditional indigenous ingredients. Local food favorites vary from one region to the next. In the cold climate of the highlands, potatoes are the staple. Dishes in the lowlands and Amazon basin tend to be more varied, incorporating many different vegetables, fruits, and fish.

Meat dishes prepared with beef, lamb, and poultry are popular among Bolivians. Llama meat is a traditional part of highland cuisine. One of the favorite meat dishes is *empanadas tucumanas*. Cooks use a mixture of beef or chicken, peas, boiled eggs, carrots, and spices, and a selection of sauces. The ingredients are deep-fried in a shell of bread dough. *Anticuchos* are a popular nighttime snack. These kebabs are made of grilled cow heart seasoned with a spicy peanut sauce and served with potatoes. *Chicharrón* are fatty, deep-fried ribs of pork cooked in beer and served with a heaping of Bolivian

Anticuchos are often sold from carts on the street.

Golden brown buñuelos are a delicious snack.

Bolivian Buñuelos

Buñuelos are a popular snack in Bolivia. While buñuelos are year-round favorites, they are traditionally eaten on Christmas morning with syrup and hot chocolate. Have an adult help you with this recipe.

Ingredients

4 cups flour

1 teaspoon baking powder

1 teaspoon salt

½ cup sugar

2 eggs

1 cup milk

4 tablespoons melted butter

Oil (for frying)

Mixture of cinnamon and sugar

Directions

In a large bowl, mix the flour, baking powder, salt, and sugar. In a smaller bowl, beat the eggs and milk together. Slowly add this to the flour mixture. Add the melted butter and beat to make the dough. Place the dough on a surface that has been floured and form it into the shape of small balls. Flatten the balls with the palm of your hand. Fry in hot oil until golden. Remove the fried dough balls and drain them on paper towels. Roll the balls in the cinnamon-and-sugar mixture. Serve warm or at room temperature.

corn. For a tasty lunch meal, Bolivians enjoy a *sandwich de chola*. This hearty mini-feast is a sandwich filled with roasted pork, pickled vegetables, and a spicy chili sauce.

Soups and stews are enjoyed throughout Bolivia. *Sopa de mani* is a traditional favorite in Cochabamba. It is made with beef ribs or chicken, peanuts, spices, and a variety of vegetables, including carrots, green beans, peas, and bell peppers. *Fricase* is a pork stew, heavily spiced with black pepper, onion, cumin, oregano, and cayenne pepper.

Bolivia offers a wide selection of fruits. These include many that are not commonly found elsewhere: *achacha*, which is both sweet and bitter, the tree tomato, and the lima, a cross between a lemon and lime. *Tumbo*, which is related to the passion fruit, has a tart flavor, and is usually made into a juice blended with sugar and water.

Many different kinds of fruits and vegetables are for sale at markets in Bolivia.

National Holidays

January 1	New Year's Day
January 22	Plurinational State Foundation Day
February or March	Carnival
March or April	Good Friday
May 1	Labor Day
May or June	Corpus Christi
June 21	Aymara New Year
August 6	Independence Day
November 2	All Souls' Day
December 25	Christmas Day

Dessert lovers enjoy *budín de quinoa*, a pudding made with quinoa, honey, and raisins. It is a favorite in the highland cities of La Paz and Oruro. *Cuñapé* is a baked dessert made with tapioca flour. It is crispy on the outside and has melted soft cheese on the inside.

Carnival

Carnivals are the grandest displays in Bolivian life. Most Bolivian carnivals occur on Catholic holidays. The most famous is held in Oruro in late February or early March in the week leading up to Lent, a solemn period that precedes Easter.

The celebration is a blending of Catholic and indigenous rituals and imagery. The Carnival begins with a colorful parade featuring people dressed as devils, pumas, condors, and monkeys, all symbols of indigenous mythology. Thousands of dancers dressed in brilliantly colored costumes and headwear weave through the streets. Bands playing horns, drums, guitars, and flutes accompany the dancers. The most famous

folk dance is La Diablada (Dance of the Devils), which represents the triumph of good over evil. The victory, acted out by masked dancers in demonic costumes, symbolizes the struggle of indigenous peoples against the Spanish colonial rulers. Today, Bolivians of many different ethnic backgrounds come together to celebrate their independence and their unique cultural traditions.

Timeline

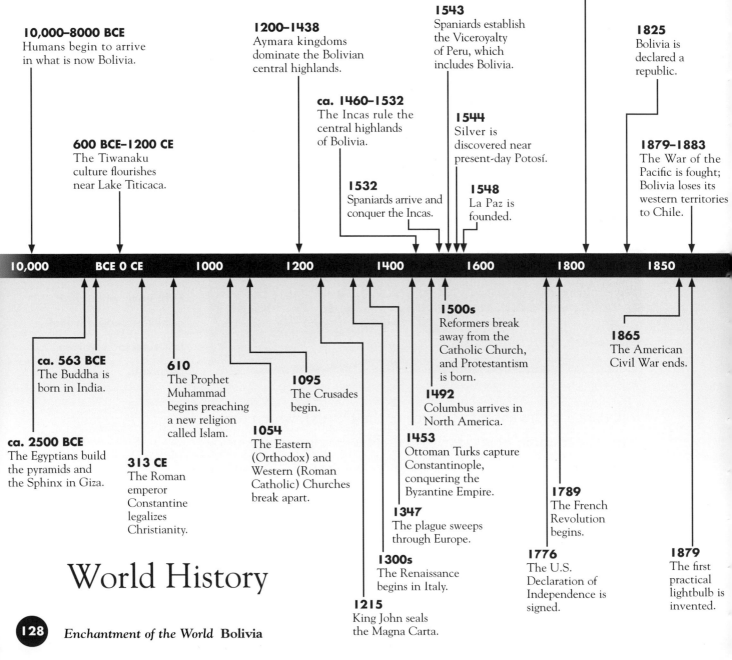

Bolivian History

10,000–8000 BCE
Humans begin to arrive in what is now Bolivia.

600 BCE–1200 CE
The Tiwanaku culture flourishes near Lake Titicaca.

1200–1438
Aymara kingdoms dominate the Bolivian central highlands.

ca. 1460–1532
The Incas rule the central highlands of Bolivia.

1532
Spaniards arrive and conquer the Incas.

1543
Spaniards establish the Viceroyalty of Peru, which includes Bolivia.

1544
Silver is discovered near present-day Potosí.

1548
La Paz is founded.

1809
Bolivia proclaims independence from Spain.

1825
Bolivia is declared a republic.

1879–1883
The War of the Pacific is fought; Bolivia loses its western territories to Chile.

10,000	BCE 0 CE	1000	1200	1400	1600	1800	1850

World History

ca. 2500 BCE
The Egyptians build the pyramids and the Sphinx in Giza.

ca. 563 BCE
The Buddha is born in India.

313 CE
The Roman emperor Constantine legalizes Christianity.

610
The Prophet Muhammad begins preaching a new religion called Islam.

1054
The Eastern (Orthodox) and Western (Roman Catholic) Churches break apart.

1095
The Crusades begin.

1215
King John seals the Magna Carta.

1300s
The Renaissance begins in Italy.

1347
The plague sweeps through Europe.

1453
Ottoman Turks capture Constantinople, conquering the Byzantine Empire.

1492
Columbus arrives in North America.

1500s
Reformers break away from the Catholic Church, and Protestantism is born.

1776
The U.S. Declaration of Independence is signed.

1789
The French Revolution begins.

1865
The American Civil War ends.

1879
The first practical lightbulb is invented.

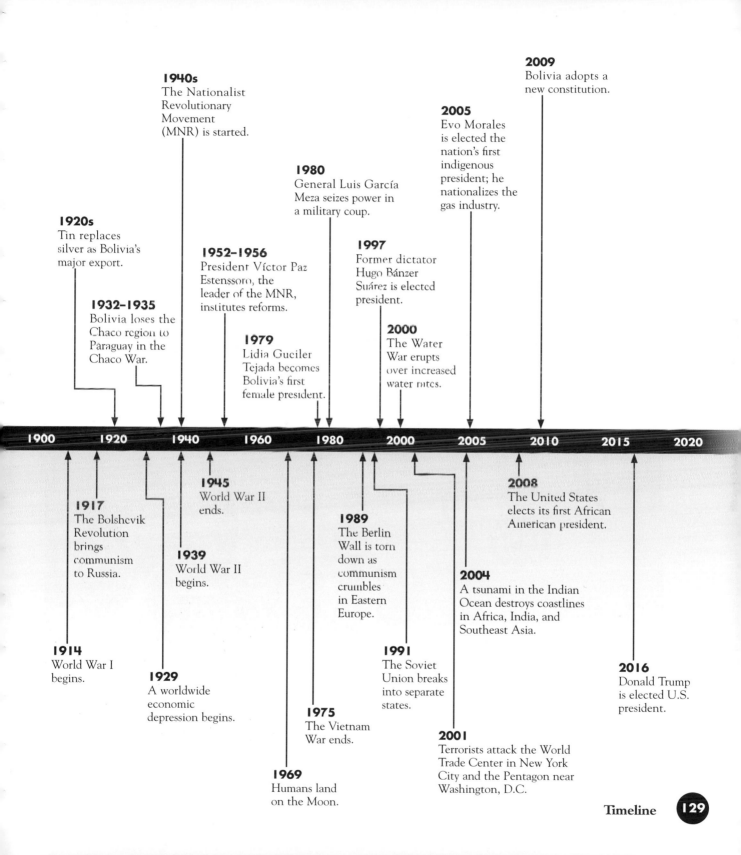

2009
Bolivia adopts a new constitution.

1940s
The Nationalist Revolutionary Movement (MNR) is started.

2005
Evo Morales is elected the nation's first indigenous president; he nationalizes the gas industry.

1980
General Luis García Meza seizes power in a military coup.

1920s
Tin replaces silver as Bolivia's major export.

1952–1956
President Víctor Paz Estenssoro, the leader of the MNR, institutes reforms.

1997
Former dictator Hugo Bánzer Suárez is elected president.

1932–1935
Bolivia loses the Chaco region to Paraguay in the Chaco War.

1979
Lidia Gueiler Tejada becomes Bolivia's first female president.

2000
The Water War erupts over increased water rates.

1900   1920   1940   1960   1980   2000   2005   2010   2015   2020

1945
World War II ends.

1917
The Bolshevik Revolution brings communism to Russia.

1939
World War II begins.

1989
The Berlin Wall is torn down as communism crumbles in Eastern Europe.

2008
The United States elects its first African American president.

1914
World War I begins.

1929
A worldwide economic depression begins.

1991
The Soviet Union breaks into separate states.

2004
A tsunami in the Indian Ocean destroys coastlines in Africa, India, and Southeast Asia.

2016
Donald Trump is elected U.S. president.

1975
The Vietnam War ends.

1969
Humans land on the Moon.

2001
Terrorists attack the World Trade Center in New York City and the Pentagon near Washington, D.C.

Timeline   **129**

Fast Facts

Official name: Plurinational State of Bolivia

Capitals: Sucre is the official capital and the judicial capital; La Paz is the seat of the executive and legislative branches of government

Official languages: Spanish, Quechua, and Aymara

Official religion: None

Year of founding: 1825

National anthem: "Bolivianos, el Hado Propicio" ("Bolivians, a Most Favorable Destiny")

Type of government: Presidential republic

Head of state: President

Head of government: President

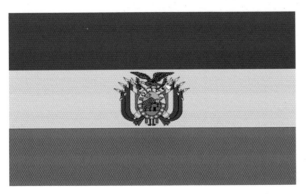

Left to right: **National flag, protesters**

PERU

Cobija ○   ○ Riberalta

BRAZIL

Madidi N.P.

Noel Kempff
Mercado N.P.

○ San Borja   ○ Trinidad

Lake
Titicaca
○ Puerto Acosta
Tiwanaku   ○ Achacachi
Guaqui   La Paz
Coro Coro ○   El Alto
Coro Coro

BOLIVIA

Cochabamba ○   ○ Punata
Ururó ○
○ Aiquile
Isallavi ○   ○ Llallagua
Chipaya ○   Sucre ⚙ ○ Tarabuco
Cal Orcko
Potosí ○
○ Camiri

Isiboro Sécure N.P.
and Indigenous Territory

San Juan de Yapacaní
Santa Cruz

○ Vallegrande
○ Roboré

Kaa-Iya del
Gran Chaco N.P.

PACIFIC
OCEAN

Uyuni ○

Aguaragüe
N.P.   ○ Villamontes
Tupiza ○   ○ Tarija

CHILE

Eduardo Avaroa
Andean Fauna Nat'l. Reserve

ARGENTINA

PARAGUAY

NORTH
AMERICA

Area of map   SOUTH
AMERICA

0   200 MI
0   200 KM

Cacti

Area of country:	424,164 square miles (1,098,580 sq km)
Bordering countries:	Brazil to the north and east; Paraguay and Argentina to the south; Chile and Peru to the west
Highest elevation:	Mount Sajama, 21,463 feet (6,542 m) above sea level
Lowest elevation:	Southeastern border with Paraguay, 295 feet (90 m) above sea level
Hottest average temperature:	86°F (30°C) in the Chaco lowlands
Lowest average temperature:	48°F (9°C) in the highlands
Average annual precipitation:	39 to 157 inches (100 to 400 cm) in the tropical lowlands; 8 to 31 inches (20 to 79 cm) in the highlands

National population (2018 est.):	11,217,864	
Population of major cities (2012):	Santa Cruz	1,453,549
	El Alto	848,840
	La Paz	764,617
	Cochabamba	630,587
	Oruro	264,683

Landmarks:
- ▶ *Immaculate Conception Cathedral*, Concepción
- ▶ *Jesuit Missions of Chiquitos*, Santa Cruz
- ▶ *Madidi National Park*, La Paz Department
- ▶ *Salar de Uyuni*, the Altiplano
- ▶ *Witches' Market*, La Paz

Economy: Bolivia has an abundance of mineral resources. Oil and natural gas exports—primarily to Brazil and Argentina—account for about half of Bolivia's total exports. Bolivia is one of the world's largest exporters of tin. Silver, zinc, lead, tungsten, potassium, and lithium are also mined. Many different crops including potatoes, corn, and coffee are grown in Bolivia. Cattle and llamas are among the many kinds of livestock Bolivians raise. Major manufactured products in Bolivia include foods and chemical products.

Currency: The boliviano. In 2018, 1 boliviano equaled 14¢, and 6.93 bolivianos equaled $1.

System of weights and measures: The metric system is the official system of measurement, but some old Spanish measures are used in marketplaces.

Literacy rate: 92%

Common Spanish words and phrases:

Hola	Hello
Buenos días	Good morning
Buenas tardes	Good evening
¿Cómo estás?	How are you?
Gracias	Thank you
De nada	You're welcome
¿Cómo te llamas?	What is your name?
¿Cuánto?	How much?
¿Dónde está . . . ?	Where is . . . ?
¿Hablas inglés?	Do you speak English?
Me llamo . . .	My name is . . .
Sí	Yes

Prominent Bolivians:	Atahualpa	(1502–1533)
	Inca king	
	Lidia Gueiler Tejada	(1921–2011)
	President	
	Jaime Laredo	(1941–)
	Violinist and conductor	
	Evo Morales	(1959–)
	President	
	Melchor Pérez de Holguín	(ca. 1660–1725)
	Painter	
	Antonio José de Sucre	(1795–1830)
	Independence leader and president	
	Adela Zamudio	(1854–1928)
	Poet	

Clockwise from top: **Currency, Jaime Laredo, schoolchildren**

To Find Out More

Books

Nonfiction

▶ Cruz, Barbara C. *Simón Bolívar: Fighting for Latin American Liberation*. New York: Enslow Publishing, 2018.

▶ Montgomery, Cy. *Amazon Adventure*. Boston: Houghton Mifflin Harcourt for Young Readers, 2017.

▶ Pateman, Robert, Marcus Cramer, and Debbie Nevins. *Bolivia*. New York: Cavendish Square, 2017.

Fiction

▶ Crowder, Melanie. *An Uninterrupted View of the Sky*. New York: Philomel Books, 2017.

Music

▶ Florilegium Ens. *Bolivian Baroque*. Herwijnen, Netherlands: Channel Classics, 2005.

▶ *A Rough Guide to the Music of the Andes: Bolivia*. London: World Music Network, 2005.

▶ Visit this Scholastic website for more information on Bolivia:
www.factsfornow.scholastic.com
Enter the keyword **Bolivia**

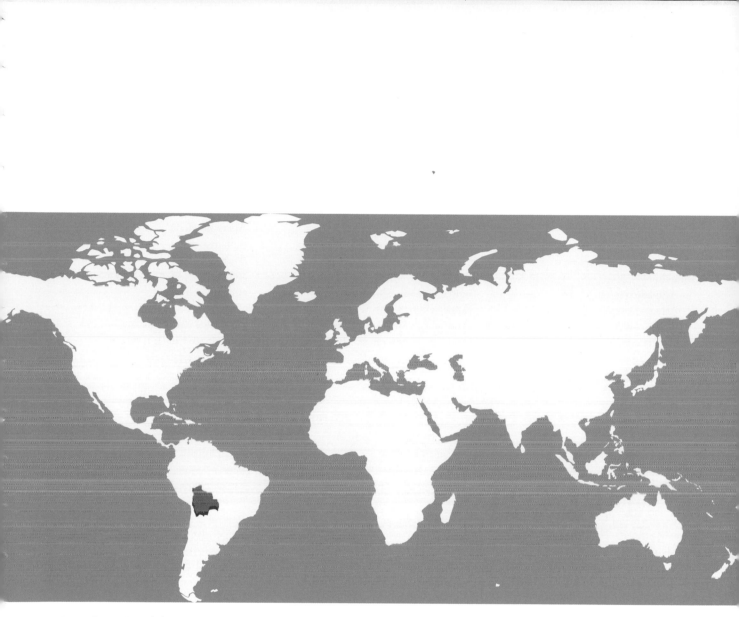

Location of Bolivia

Index

Page numbers in *italics* indicate illustrations.